Rival Gardens

TED KOOSER CONTEMPORARY POETRY | *Editor:* Ted Kooser

Rival Gardens

New and Selected Poems | CONNIE WANEK

Introduction by Ted Kooser

University of Nebraska Press | Lincoln and London

Publication of this volume was made possible in part
by the generous support of the H. Lee and Carol
Gendler Charitable Fund.

Library of Congress Cataloging-in-Publication Data

Wanek, Connie, 1952–
[Poems. Selections]
Rival gardens: new and selected poems /
Connie Wanek; introduction by Ted Kooser.
pages   cm.—(Ted Kooser contemporary poetry)
ISBN 978-0-8032-6964-4 (paperback)
ISBN 978-0-8032-8506-4 (epub)
ISBN 978-0-8032-8507-1 (mobi)
ISBN 978-0-8032-8508-8 (pdf)
I. Title.
PS3573.A47686A6 2016
811'.54—dc23
2015032075

Set in Monotype Fournier by L. Auten.

For Phil

Contents

....

Selections from
On Speaking Terms

Acknowledgments

Poems selected from *Bonfire* and *Hartley Field* are reprinted by permission of Connie Wanek. Thanks to New Rivers Press for publishing *Bonfire* (1997), and to Holy Cow! Press for publishing *Hartley Field* (2002). Poems from *On Speaking Terms* (2010) are reprinted by gracious permission of Copper Canyon Press.

The author wishes to thank the following journals and collections in which the poems selected from *Bonfire*, *Hartley Field*, and *On Speaking Terms* first appeared, a few in slightly different versions: *Artword Quarterly, Ascent, Atlantic Monthly, Bloomsbury Review, Briar Cliff Review, Cafe Solo, Country Journal, Flurry, Great River Review, Green Mountains Review, Loonfeather, Luna, Minnesota Monthly, Minnesota Poetry Calendar, Narrative, Negative Capability, North Coast Review, North Country Sampler, Plainsong, Poetry, Poetry East, Prairie Schooner, Puerto del Sol, Quarterly West, Rhino, River Oak Review, Ruby, Seattle Review, Shared Visions, Speakeasy, Tarpaulin Sky, The Talking of Hands, Texas Observer, To Topio, Turtle, Virginia Quarterly Review, Water-Stone Review, Willow Review, Wolf Head Quarterly.*

Many thanks also to the following journals and collections in which the new poems were first published: BILiNE, *Fog and Woodsmoke, Freshwater Review, Great River Review, Hampden-Sydney Poetry Review, Midwest Prairie Review, Narrative, New Ohio Review, Poetry East, St. Paul Almanac, Upstreet, What Light, Water-Stone Review.*

Special gratitude to the newspaper column American Life in Poetry and to the radio program *The Writer's Almanac* for presenting poems that appear in this volume. Also thanks to the Arrowhead Regional Arts Council, the Jerome Foundation, the Loft Literary Center, the Minnesota State Arts Board, and the Witter Bynner Foundation for their important and very kind support.

Introduction

It may be a common though rarely acknowledged fate for a literary artist to discover to his embarrassment that he likes somebody else's work a good deal more than his own, but that's the way I've felt about the art of Connie Wanek during the dozen or more years since I first heard her read her poems at a conference in Duluth. I was seated that day next to Carol Bly, whose judgment about quality was never less than impeccable, and she agreed with me about the marvelously inventive, richly associative, and deeply moving poetry we were hearing. I wish that Carol could have lived to see the book you're holding now.

In 2005, while I was serving as U.S. poet laureate, I presented one of two prestigious Witter Bynner Fellowships to Connie, who with her husband, Phil, drove from Minnesota to Washington to accept the award and to read her poems into the archives of the Library of Congress. There were Connie and I, both from the vast middle section of our country, an area that literary critics from both coasts avoid as if it were Death Valley in July, the two of us in the library's handsome Poetry Room, a little parlor with furniture one is afraid to sit on and a guest book that Robert Frost had signed over and over again as if to underline that he'd been there.

And there we were, later that day, flanked by dusty velvet curtains on the stage of the stately Coolidge Auditorium, where scores of important American writers had stood to accept their honors and applause. I don't know about Connie, but I had the time of my life that afternoon, being able to recognize this immensely talented poet who was not a professor of creative writing on her way to a better position but a person who worked at a public library and, with her husband, fixed up old houses for resale, a part-time painter and decorator, a gardener, a full-time mother, and a journeyman framing carpenter of our beautiful American language.

I hope you've bought this book because it's something to keep and read over and over again, but if you've borrowed it from your public library or from a friend, I'm just as pleased. Among these pages are dozens of poems that offer an indelible language to use while admiring our world.

·

Rival Gardens

Selections from *Bonfire*

April

When the snowbank dissolved
I found a comb and a muddy quarter.
I found the corpse of that missing mitten
still clutching some snow.

Then came snow with lightning,
beauty with a temper.
And sleet, the compromise that pleases no one;
precipitation by committee.

Out on Lake Superior the worried ice
paces up and down the shoreline
wearing itself out.

Chimneys have given up smoking.
In the balcony of the woods,
a soprano with feathers.

And upon the creek
the wicked spell is broken.
You are free to be water now.
You are free to go.

Red Fox

He lived all summer on the great man's estate,
the red fox, like a concubine.
The sight of him taking the bait
made the old gentleman tremble —
his modest toilette at the fountain
observed through binoculars,
his unmolested naps near the gray rock
where sunlight streamed through a dying birch.

Over and over the fox saw the old man hobble out
and fill the meat bowl. His was a pungent,
almost medical smell, that clung
like a tendril to the complicated air of human places.
At first each nerve objected. The fox
saw two dogs at the bay window, watching,
their coarse, domesticated faces
full of eager malevolence, like ex-wives.

Then overnight the sumac turned red.
The creeper suddenly blushed at its own rapaciousness.
How hard the wind tried to pick the trees up
but leaves only came away.
That summer, like all the others,
fled while the old man still wanted it, and the fox, too,
vanished into the copper-colored undergrowth
as into the magician's sleeve.

Abstract

The story begins a hundred years ago,
notations in that fine antique hand,
the getting and losing of a piece of land
ending with us.

Two wives became widows in this house,
walked from window to window looking out,
shrinking in their dresses,
padding their shoes with Kleenex.
The lake was always there, the fog climbed the hill,
and the moon grew stout and thin
per the promissory note.

Teeth fell out, there was a divorce
(Solvieg got the house),
and at last the two children who fought so bitterly
had to "divide by equal shares, share and share alike"
the southerly 100 feet of lot 9 Endion Subdivision
together with all improvements.

It was the sister who stayed on.
It was she who saw the peonies through the dry year,
who took the broom to the wasp nest in the soffit,
who embraced those endless domestic economies,
and who penciled into the margins
padlock combinations, paint colors,
the Latin names of her perennials.

Her bones grew hollow like a bird's
so that when it was time to fly
she had only to spread her old wool shawl
and drop the ballast of this abstract.

Wild Apples

The tree is old, hidden behind
a veil of Virginia creeper,
the apples astringent, misshapen,
green with red tiger stripes,
misguided adornment or miracle
in the logged-over third or fourth or fifth growth
along the creek. I gather a few windfalls,
too hard to bruise,
as I pass from nowhere to nowhere.

If I had roots I would put them down here.
Living roots, roots with feeling.
The apples are placed on the windowsill
where they can see out —
morning windows, sun coming out of the woods, disentangled.
How freely it floats before the clouds,
then willingly enters them.
And my daughter, scowling all day,
how she smiles when her friends come for her.

The hard brown boys find the apple tree
on one of their patrols
and load up on ammo.
One apple penetrates the storm window
but not the sash, and so glass separates
the curiously reunited offspring of the tree —
the litter brought together as dogs —
while the boys have of course scattered,
careening downhill on their bent bicycles.

The unburdened tree stands straighter,
smoothing the wrinkled skirt.
After all these years, some time apparently remains,
another evening, another autumn,
a tender half-inch of growth on each arthritic branch.
Apples lie soft and brown in the underbrush,
waste and redundancy, windowsill apples
sitting on their weeping mold.

Once you took my picture under this very tree.
I was holding the child, who was holding wild apples.
Fourteen months, I wrote on the back.
She and I both looked pale after that first intense year,
milky, like the edge of the sky,
slightly translucent, slightly grave.
She was mine. She didn't belong to herself then.
It was September, just as it is now,
the sun listing to the south,
the hill's shadow crossing me at the knee.

The Girl and the Horses

I woke to find the gate open and the horses gone
and I thought, "What haven't I given you?"
Dawn was drying the gravel on the road;
the bridle I carried clinked against my knee.
They hadn't gone far. They stood at the corner
where the road turned toward infinite places
and raised their heads from their grazing to watch me.
I walked toward them, falsely confident,
like a teacher, unable to disguise
the nature of my duty.

The big roan played a vital part in my success,
turning his ears forward as he smelled sugar,
two white, pure, perfect cubes. And then,
because he had so often done so, he accepted the bit.
I drew him out of the ditch, two legs leading four,
seventy pounds leading seven hundred,
and the other horses, sighing and snorting, followed.
It looked as if we'd been on some field trip,
saw how money was made, or how trees
are stripped and turned into toilet paper.

That morning I thought myself lucky
and the beasts immeasurably foolish
as I led them back. All in, the gate locked,
I pulled the roan's head down to me
and slipped the bridle off, and he nipped me,
nipped me with his huge teeth, yellow as corn,
near my ear, and bolted into the pasture.

Daylilies

If these yellow daylilies
made the sound suggested by their anatomy
we couldn't have them in the garden —
great gold horns
on stems that would support them,
like some stage mother, on a world tour.
But they're rooted here in the red clay,
noisy only by virtue of their color
and posture, that desperate leaning away
from the leaves, that sun hunger.

Perhaps they know they have only one day.
One cool morning, a wind off the lake,
and one noon under a sun
that returns the most ardent affection.
One evening watching the shadows
of the porch spindles lengthen without tangling,
and the day is done. A day
that might have been worse or better,
that was never ours alone
though it seemed so.

The Wandering Sky

It's the wind that drives the sky to one side
and herds the stars along, and pulls
the thread out of the needle.
A lifetime frugally spent
but gone all the same, and the chair
that has become your tame little horse
tethered beneath the wandering sky.
The grandchildren dash through the room
like comets leaving a brilliant trail.
They have left the door wide open
but the wind will close it.

Wherever we go the clouds have preceded us.
Clouds of the vast transformation.
Thin clouds that thinly cross the bald dome.
Clouds like fish bones, like ribs
protecting the lung of the atmosphere.
Sometimes there are long words in the sky,
a sentence finished beyond the horizon.

Broom

A blossom on its long stem
the broom is a hag of a tulip.
It is a woman who ties back
her hair with wire,
who wears burlap,
who eats clay.

For its fidelity
the broom has been granted
the ability to carry the witch
to the clouds. Who was the first
to slip it between her legs
and vanish?

Skim Milk

The weary cow barely made the barn
and the farmer cleaned her withered udder
with little hope; but lo, a few drops,
a cupful, and at last a carton
of this Spartan beverage—
tempting, as self-flagellation is tempting.

Skim milk, reconstituted perhaps
from the dried granules, the little milk seeds
we distribute to developing nations
when what they need is pure butterfat
that lines the soul like a nest,
that recalls the sun, summer meadows . . .
buttercups . . . butterflies . . .

Forget summer. The doctor hands you a stern menu
and the brilliant little lamps of pleasure
burn out one by one, irreplaceable.
Years stretch ahead, lean and dim,
like so many glasses of skim milk,
and the sad old cow looks up sympathetically,
her mouth full of thistles.

Radish

In this cold clay thrives a hot little vegetable,
the radish, the sensualist. When you wash it,
letting water trickle over its swollen root,
you make it very happy.

When you're dull, pull half a dozen.
They're crowded anyway,
gaining weight on all this rain.
Eat them red and plain.

Or eat them sliced and white.
Bite them and they bite you back—
you like that; resistance sharpens the appetite.
Attribute this blush to the effect of radishes.

Radiator

Mittens are drying on the radiator
boots nearby, one on its side.
Like some monstrous segmented insect
the radiator elongates under the window.

Or it is a beast with many shoulders
domesticated in the Ice Age.
How many years it takes
to move from room to room!

Some cage their radiators
but this is unnecessary
as they have little desire to escape.

Like turtles they are quite self-contained.
If they seem sad, it is only the same sadness
we all feel, unlovely, slowly growing cold.

Missed Bus

He sprinted around the corner to see it depart,
the flatulent yellow bus,
its windows inhabited by smug, successful faces.
A few noticed him,
his coat unzipped and only one mitten,
standing in a cloud of his own breath.
Failure is complete only when it is witnessed.

A little snow, so light it seemed not to fall
but to drift down, sideways, and up too,
pausing inquiringly before his eyes.
Perhaps the snow would eventually
end up on the ground. Or perhaps
it would be called back at the last moment
by a mother who insists
on a kiss in the middle of chaos.

The bus moves through the blue morning
lit up like a traveling theater,
a shadow puppet in every window.
It always seems they are all against you,
shouting to the driver
"Leave! Leave! He's almost here!"

Duluth, Minnesota

A moose has lost his way
amidst the human element downtown,
the old-timers waiting out January
at the bar, the realtors and bureaucrats
with their identical plumage
(so that you must consult your Roger Tory Peterson)
hopping up the steps of City Hall
eating Hansel's bread crumbs —
poor moose, a big male who left
his antlers somewhere in the woods.
He keeps checking his empty holster . . .

People suffer the winters
for this kind of comedy.
Spectators climb the snowbanks,
dogs bark, the moose lowers
his shaggy head, his grave eyes
reminiscent somehow of Abe Lincoln.
Firemen, police, reporters, DNR,
two cents' worth from every quarter,
till the moose lopes down Fourth Street
toward St. Mary's Hospital Emergency Entrance
and slips into an alley.

Later, the same moose — it must be —
is spotted farther up the hillside.
It's a mixed neighborhood; a moose
isn't terribly out of place.
And when he walks calmly up behind
one old man shoveling his driveway,
the Duluthian turns without surprise.
"*Two blocks east,*" he says,
"*Then you'll hit a small creek that will take you
to Chester Park, and right into the woods.*"
He adds, "*Good luck, now.*"

Blue Moon

for the sisters Jacobson

This August a complete restoration, a blue moon.
It hesitates when it sees all of us
gathered here, watching. What can I do,
it says, but simply rise —

The day was so fair, so blond,
and the great lake becalmed, inviting
a hardy swimmer and his dog.
Inside the body the heart throbbed
like an engine of Swedish manufacture,
strong enough for a second lifetime.

A single cloud made the sky seem bluer,
one cloud against such odds.
True, we seldom see a day so unblemished,
so childish, so soon over.
Let us meet on the rocky shore
to ask this rare, self-conscious moon
to intercede on our behalf.

The lake lifts and sinks
like a sleeping father's chest, so gently
that small craft venture forth.
The stars, too, sense no danger in the heavens.
Our small fire burns only the sticks we give it;
we have that much control.
The moon returns with no assurances
but spreads a little light on the footpath.

The Gelding

As I recall, the black horse just appeared,
undelivered, unrequested,
dusty and skinny, like a tramp
with his hat in his good hand.
He was used to pity. He could work with it.

His dull eyes were rimmed with red,
and his habits were all bad:
he bit, suddenly and cruelly,
with his ears back flat.
He kicked the yearling squarely
in the ribs, so thoroughly
did he despise innocence.
The sweet filly he tried to mount
there, in the pasture, knowing we watched.
And we added to his scars
as everyone who owned him did.

Only once I forced him to take the bit
and slipped onto his bony back.
He seemed to acquiesce, then
threw himself into the fence.

If an animal can't be used one way
it will be used another.
So they came for him,
four strong men, armed with cigarettes,
leather, rope, a blindfold,
in a truck barred like a jail.
The black horse fought as if
he smelled a place they'd been.
Trussed in, he was at last becalmed.
Almost bored. The truck rumbled away,
blue exhaust drifting into the cornfield.

Dragonfly

A dragonfly visits me as I take down the laundry.
He clings to a sleeve like a mighty cuff link,
gold and purple, with four sluggish wings
the shape of willow leaves, and will not fly.
No, he has found the last sun
that stains the garment and the day, and will not fly.

Night stands with its goods at the door,
impatient to inhabit summer's mansion,
like the unsentimental purchaser on closing day.
You lead him through the empty rooms a last time
and give him the key. Somewhere a window left open —
and the cold rushes in.

The moon seems always in the sky, night or day.
All life ends under such a fierce moon,
sharp tipped as an Abyssinian sword.
What are your thoughts, dragonfly,
as my finger comes so near?
Do you feel the furnace of my red blood?
Can you trust me? I could put you in a jar
decorated with clematis, a pleasant room,
a windowsill, a button to push for the nurse.
But no, you seem to say no,
as you throw yourself into the grass.
I see worn places on your wings
just as every leaf in the woods
has its caterpillar hole.

After our talk, we let each other go.
In a few steps I enter the shadow of the house
that rises on me like a watermark.
All over the sky the nighthawks
are crossing through the visible spectrum.
And the day, like a last penny
pulled from deep in the pocket, is spent.

Rain

When the rain comes
you don't try to stop it.
You don't give it a final warning.
It comes, and the plants look up
and hold up their leaves.

It is the age of parents failing,
asleep in the afternoon, awake in the night.
The first light enters the east window
trying to make the nerves come alive
like leaves growing from a stump.

When the grandchildren visit
each must suffer an inspection, a silly joke
and the reverent touch of the old hands —
how hard it is to love and be loved!

Rain, come out of the milky sky
and wash the dust from the bird wings!
There is no reason for anything
yet we live.

Toward Dusk

My hand on the gate
I look back into the garden.
My shadow lingers between the rows
and pulls the shadow of a weed.

The seedlings are thick stemmed,
well begun. Should I not return
they would still grow, these delphiniums,
blue eyed, my height and a little beyond.

It wasn't my fate after all
to do more than plant
at the proper phase of the moon,
and love what grows.

Peonies

It is winter before we think clearly
of the peonies. Wind rearranges
a light snow over their roots,
filling the faint tracks of the neighbor's cat.
The wind has forgotten why it feels so unhappy.

I remember that mild June night
we sat out waiting for the moon,
and fireflies appeared, like broken pieces of it
drifting over the peonies.
The flowers had a light of their own
and regarded the world as infants do,
full of great, unknown capacity.

The white peony was cooler than the air.
When I took it in my hand
and held it near your face
I saw your unguarded, nocturnal features,
simple and irrational.
I believed then in what cannot be touched.

The sun rose on peonies
throwing away their petals
as nuns conceal their hair and bodies.
They had served their short time
in the physical world.
Now it is the snow that falls
in great soft petals, spent blossoms
on the year's darkest day.

Amaryllis

A flower needs to be this size
to conceal the winter window,
and this color, the red
of a Fiat with the top down,
to impress us, dull as we've grown.

Months ago the gigantic onion of a bulb
half above the soil
stuck out its green tongue
and slowly, day by day,
the flower itself entered our world,

closed, like hands that captured a moth,
then open, as eyes open,
and the amaryllis, seeing us,
was somehow undiscouraged.
It stands before us now

as we eat our soup;
you pour a little of your drinking water
into its saucer, and a few crumbs
of fragrant earth fall
onto the tabletop.

Christmas Tree

Five days after Christmas
we are weary of the tree.
Stale joy, a half-grown puppy.
No one waters it
or admires the lights;
the sharp spruce needles
drop onto the tree skirt,
through the holy chamber
the presents occupied, empty now,
things eaten and broken and read,
Christmas past. The ornaments,
gaudy and plain, are folded and stacked,
and the tree stands as it once did,
but dead. It's lovely anyway by itself,
like an empty house. Walking through
you notice wall shadows, door handles,
the hall floor like a river of oak,
and the windows, what is free to go out
and what is admitted at each pane of glass.
You notice your noisy shoes
and your enthusiastic, unnatural voice.
We own too much.

I am cleaning the old man's house.
Nothing of value. In the attic
boxes of Christmas decorations
the heirs do not wish to examine:
"Give it all to the poor."
Umbrellas lean in the corners,
the closets an impenetrable mass
of worthless retainees, the squalid pantry,
the predictably unclean bath—

but in the basement, jars of screws
arranged like a surgeon's tray
and a magnificent shortwave,
his audio window. Toward the end
the eyes always do fail.

We admire the tree anew, for one moment,
before dragging it into the snow.
Bitter cold is the forecast, dangerous windchills,
one hundred percent chance of snow.
The tree will not suffer.
Wind will build a drift
over its northern branches, a pale, cold wall
rising, with little windows on the east.
Some creature may fly through these windows
which are always left open.
And here in the corner where the tree stood,
a chair, a lamp, a wastebasket.

January

1.

Close the book. Close the blinds.
Close the door tight till the handle clicks.
Inside a walnut a white worm
gnaws whatever touches it.
The rooms are warm for the sick one,
in every corner the smell of fever.
We are nearly out of batteries.
Between us we have twenty pale fingers
to count each hour of the dark.

It is said the sun rises,
yes, like air trapped under the ice.
We can see it through the low clouds,
but it doesn't matter.
The winter is rich and we are poor—
yet the cold comes in
to finger the thin curtains.

2.

When I close my eyes
I see them clearly, the bathers
wading near the dock in the weedy water.
Behind them the summer hillside,
the pedigreed birches, popple
thriving like mongrels. I see them
clearly, the youngest up to her waist,
the mother standing at the water's edge
shading her eyes. I hear her thin call.
The older siblings, the boy and girl
who look so much alike at this age,
have undertaken a quest for minnows.
And what would you do with them?

Let them go. Capture them and let them go.
Hold them in the palm, have them,
and see that they feel as you would,
held under. They are like tiny
individual muscles. Their lips are transparent.
The flared gills dry like petals.
Drop them quickly so you can breathe again.

No one wants to sleep.
Raindrops splash on the lake
like handfuls of minnows.
The children feel feverish with sunburn,
sand in the creases behind their knees.
For hours the warm twilight
lingers in the woods, while
we sit on the porch in our white pajamas
like a cluster of mushrooms.
Someone speaks aloud the word *winter*
but no one believes in such a thing.
The darkness is so shy
it has stolen away before we wake.

Bonfire

After a simple meal, we wash with snow
and throw the bones on the bonfire.
Someone drags forward the remains
of the Christmas tree . . . rags, a suitcase,
a marriage certificate. Then you rush close
and offer something from your pocket.
The great animal in the fire
stands on its hind legs
and rakes the air as it falls backwards.

The orange light is like
a scrap of cellophane over the scene,
sealing the exotic diorama:
the vast flames on this bitter January night,
and our hulking, primitive shapes
shifting, thrusting forth a long stick,
falling back as the bundle of manuscripts
at last has some effect.

Our faces, bearded and smooth,
darken as the fire dies, and the cold
clamp tightens on the little clearing.
Despite the new year, the heavens
use the same worn calendar.
But tonight, strange unreasonable hopes
stir in us like seeds planted
far in advance of the season.
What we have done so far isn't much,
but there is still time.

Ski Tracks

He left the trail here
heading for home as the crow flies—
ski tracks, one melody, one harmony,
and his meandering husky.
Straight through the brown ferns
past the sumac's red seed heads—
a little art nouveau
in the otherwise minimalist landscape.

Is this silence or exhaustion?
His skis lean against the cabin as snowflakes
drift through the porch light like moths.
This man is thin as a ski.
He boils fish and potatoes
that rise up as he stirs them
as if it is they who will be fed.

The stars look down hungrily
from their overpopulated sky
and sparks fly up from the chimney
equally unsatisfied.

2.

He built this cabin when his father died.
With the insurance money.
His wife left him when he quit his job.
"Don't keep in touch."
The gray in his beard
grew to resemble animal markings.
He thought of the woods as perfectly indifferent
then realized they were slightly irritated:
he was worse than a moose but
better than army worms.

Once he snowshoed out to the bar
and spent the night in an upstairs room.
He kept waking up. A car.
A barking dog. Even the phone lines
made a kind of whine. And that smell
of beer on the short-napped carpet.
And the floor that gave a little with each step.

Sometime in the night the weather changed.
Heavy clouds, but warmer. Rotting snow.
Yes, it was like something once alive
once swirling like a skirt.
Now his snowshoes sank into the snow's corpse.
He tried to think of it as the opposite of death,
the water released like the genie out of the bottle.
He felt the clouds sinking.
It was warm enough to rain.

Selections from *Hartley Field*

The Coin Behind Your Ear

Before you knew you owned it
it was gone, stolen, and you were a fool.
How you never felt it is the wonder,
heavy and thick,
lodged deep in your hair like a burr.
You still see the smile of the magician
as he turned the coin in his long fingers
which had so disturbed your ear
with their caress. You watched him
lift it into the light, bright as frost,
and slip it into his maze of pockets.
You felt vainly behind your ear
but there was no second coin,
nothing to tempt him back.
No one cared to know why he did it,
only how.

The Ventriloquist

He had been so lonely.
Days passed without the need to speak.
He understood at last
why God had made a man of the very dust.

It was a wooden woman
who came then into his arms.
He turned her face toward his own
and bid her speak.

She wasn't made precisely in his image
but she had charm.
Her eyes were skillfully painted
and she was sanded very smooth.

She could be dull, though,
and nothing she said ever surprised him.
Still, people smiled at them together.
He was definitely noticed.

Butter

Butter, like love,
seems common enough
yet has so many imitators.
I held a brick of it, heavy and cool,
and glimpsed what seemed like skin
beneath a corner of its wrap;
the décolletage revealed
a most attractive fat!

And most refined.
Not milk, not cream,
not even *crème de la crème*.
It was a delicacy that assured me
that bliss follows agitation,
that even pasture daisies
through the alchemy of four stomachs
may grace a king's table.

We have a yellow bowl near the toaster
where summer's butter grows
soft and sentimental.
We love it better for its weeping,
its nostalgia for buckets and churns
and deep stone wells,
for the press of a wooden butter mold
shaped like a swollen heart.

Peaches

I have eaten peach after peach
without hesitation or apology, and each
was a disappointment. Outwardly
they looked ideal, smooth as a pony muzzle
or pool table felt, sunset colored,
and when I held them I sensed
either their heartbeats or my own.

I overbought, too, thinking how lovely
they looked together, a troupe of California peaches
visiting Minnesota in July, the only month
they'd find palatable. I wondered what exactly
I expected of them. Flavor, I suppose.

Or I thought the stone
might offer me I can't say what,
like tea leaves or a fortune cookie,
some hint of a changed life.
Still moist, still bearing a tassel of flesh,
the stone requests a sympathetic burial;
it believes that any amicable clay, even mine,
is suitable for resurrection.

Red Rover

What courage we had,
our infantry stretched across the yard,
no shields, no swords,
no cavalry assembled behind us
calming their nervous mounts.
We had the strength of our arms,
the speed of our legs.
We had our friends and our convictions.
Opposite us, the undulating line
of children drew suddenly straight.
It was early on a summer day
but the larks fell silent.
A high voice
invoked the name Red Rover;
we could not say who said it first.
But righteousness passed through us
like current through a wire.
Or like an inaugural sip of wine
burning in our chests,
something father gave us
over our mother's earnest
protestations.

Jump Rope

There is menace
in its relentless course, round and round,
describing an ellipsoid,
an airy prison in which a young girl
is incarcerated.

Whom will she marry? Whom will she love?
The rope, like a snake,
has the gift of divination,
yet reveals only a hint, a single initial.
But what if she never misses?

Is competence its own reward?
Will the rope never strike her ankle,
love's bite? The enders turn and turn,
two-handed as their arms tire,
their enchantments exhausted.

It hurts to watch her now,
flushed and scowling,
her will stronger than her limbs,
her braids lashing her shoulders
with each small success.

Horses in Spring

Beware too much happiness!
The horses paused suspiciously before the open door,
snorting and stamping, while sunlight poured
onto the cold cement. They smelled snow
in the barn's shadow, mud along the south wall,
matted grass in the thawing pasture.
Their nostrils flared and their ears
lay back, then pricked forward, far forward,
and they stretched their elegant necks
as if the world were offering them a slice of sweet apple
or something even more pure, on an open palm.

I was just a girl and couldn't understand
how they could hesitate at the edge of something
so intoxicating. Spring's first bee flew blindly
in then out again, all impulse, no plan.
At last with a clattering of hooves
they left the barn for the bright paddock.

Even then they huddled together in their dull, thick coats,
superstitious, imagining a wrathful master
who would whip them for taking what is offered,
a master capricious as March.
I swung the heavy door closed
and climbed the fence to watch them,
the bay, the black, the pale appaloosa, and the rest.
No one had ever broken my will, forced me
into the traces; I was too young for school.
They tested the earth with their sensitive hooves
and didn't like it — too cold, too soft, too unpredictable.

Summer Night

The street lamp looks down;
it has dropped something
and spends the whole night
searching around its feet.
The rumble of a jet, and the fast road
blocks away, roaring like a cataract.
The scent of mown grass,
and of the body that mowed it.
The sidewalk, made of warm squares
heaved by maple roots,
covered with hieroglyphs in chalk.
A maple sapling, its trunk
wrapped to the knee
like the legs of a racehorse,
galloping straight up.
At dawn the prodigal sun returns
accompanied by equatorial birds
and a floral entourage.
What good has it done us to labor so
when all are rewarded?
Let the spade fall, then,
and join the feast.

Lemon

A lemon on the countertop
is a responsibility. Lemon-scented reveries
inspired its purchase; a modest investment,
yet one that now seems rash.

It was so plump, waxed and polished,
bumpers on both ends like a Volkswagen.
When I held it, it endeared itself to me;
I don't know how. A mystery of color,

as a flower draws the bee, bodily,
right down into it. Yet the lemon
was certainly retouched, like a photograph
signed love, Sunkist.

I scan the cookbooks, every recipe
beyond the likes of me. I think
of simply slicing it to flavor plain water.
At last I concede I'll end up doing nothing—

traveling, extensively perhaps,
to avoid the whole dilemma—coming home
to find the lemon hard and shrunken,
and bitter, quite impossibly bitter.

Long Nights

It's good to have poems that begin with tea and end with God.
—ROBERT BLY

A cup forgotten on the windowsill,
half full of cold tea, half of moonlight.
The rocking chair sits alone now,
its back erect and its seat ample.
There I nursed the first baby, and read
the *Alexandria Quartet*, wherein
a child was a further romance.
I still feel her in my arms, limp with sleep,
and see her heartbeat in her fontanel.
Whenever I tried to lay her in her crib
her eyes flew open. Let her cry, they said.
But I never let her cry.

My mother carried six of us,
one after the other, on her hip,
as we descended from her embrace
to our stations on the earth. She says
to this day her left hip is higher,
her left arm brutally strong,
her right infinitely dexterous.
Long were the nights she spent in labor
wrestling babies from the Creator.

Postcard: Busy Clarence Town Harbor on a Mail Boat Day

Bahamas, 1962

The red truck idles,
dripping an unknown fluid into its shadow.
The sky is full of the sea,
of clouds that left the salt of their estate
behind in the rich water.
At night we feel the anchor drag, and the whole island
drift toward the Southern Cross.
But the morning mail boat finds the dock, and dark heads
bend over fluttering paper
as the inquisitive breeze reads over a dozen shoulders.

Love is everywhere, like the sand. Whatever is old
is still to be loved,
whatever rusts, whatever falls behind on the sandy road,
the oldest hen, the pencil stub,
is still to be cared for. At noon the mail boat, low in the water,
restarts its engines:
our last words must be weightless.

Honesty

I could easily be honest
if I were certain of the truth.
You remember the day as sunny and hot,
the car an oven, the air
rippling over the green chile fields.
I remember clouds building in the western sky
as quickly as if there'd been an explosion
out where the military tested
something big and vastly expensive
over and over.

Everyone seems so confident.
Those letters to the editor: "Get real" and
"Wake up, people!" The man from Pengilly
who keeps "loaded guns in readily accessible locations."

I honestly don't know why I had children
or why I sew, or garden,
except that if it's true we're made in God's image
we are born to create, or to try—
though when you smile at my earnestness
I see that you're right, I am naive.

I remember when our daughter realized
it was possible not to tell the truth.
She was three years old.
I saw something pass over her eyes, a petit mal,
leaving a kind of bright residue,
the shimmer of a most attractive lie, a fairy tale
no one had told her, yet she suddenly knew,
about a girl who never pinched a friend
however much she deserved it.

An hour passes and I'm no longer angry,
though it's true I was.
Sunlight streams through the screen door—
a late clearing, just as you predicted.
We're together in the kitchen,
a friendly bumping as we wash and slice
the green and red, yellow and white
ingredients, and stir them all in the kettle
until nothing is exclusively itself.

Black and White Photograph

She lined up the boys by height
and steadied her camera.
All were dressed alike, in nothing
but shorts and holey tennies,
nearly bald — their hair summer shorn —
and they fidgeted as she fixed them
in the tiny window, six boys,
ribby and scabby, their limbs aboriginal brown
under the hot Iowa sun
and thin as cornstalks.
Somewhere in the black camera
it is still 1956, and mothers are hanging
diapers on the clothesline,
a practiced eye on the clouds.
It seems in each life
a moment comes that the heart adheres to,
when light floods in to assemble
a single image in the dark.

Memorial Day at the Lake

The cousins drift far out in their inflatable raft,
but the water is calm, the sun generous,
Grandpa and Grandma are still alive, luck is with us.
A new hatch of children train to be sand-artisans
while aunts and mothers tan their winter legs.
Someone discovers a tick and hysteria erupts,
inspections, tears from the youngest —
"I don't want to be eaten!"

Around the campfire, a great circle of rosy knees
as the Family solves the Poland problem, restructures welfare
and deliberates the shortcomings of the absent sister-in-law.
The men still wear their feed caps in the darkness,
and moonlight falls on the brims.
The least wind makes the young aspens nervous —
they are so sensitive. They take things so seriously.
Shouldn't they be asleep by now?

Herd the kids to bed and come back to the fire,
the voices softer now but more frank, the beer cans light.
Someone says you can't be gentle
and still be a man. You put away childish things.
You lose a finger in the combine, it's gone.
And in the flames are other fires . . . the order comes
to advance, and it makes no sense to die so far from home,
to lift up your body to a bullet. Comrades fell,
but you came back to the floating world,
to buoyant days like red and white bobbers, sleepily tended,
to fields deep with sweet alfalfa.
The price of life is of course death,
but only one death, and so many lives.

It's the morning of speedboats
and water skis and excited novices.
When it's your turn to grasp the stick
and step onto the water,
to feel the pull of a hundred horses,
then think of yourself as a water beetle,
hard on the outside, light as cork.
Someone has lent you his life jacket
and buckled it snugly over your heart.
Everyone you love is in that boat, looking back.
It's far too late to say no.
These are your people.

The Midwife

She was a medium, a fortune-teller,
or an emissary sent to God himself
to beg humbly that the child
come whole and sound
and soon. Her hands were so clean,
the nails clipped or bitten,
the skin dry and tight.
She slept off and on,
accustomed to resting when she could
in a bed or chair,
like a traveler crossing the frontier
between tragedy and comedy,
land forever claimed by both sides.
What she witnessed
was the opposite of drowning,
a reenactment of the moment
the first amphibian took a breath,
the tadpole of a child
swimming eagerly into her hands.

The Exchange

Sometimes when I see a wad of money,
half an inch of twenties,
old bills, folded and straightened,
smelling of tobacco and palm grease,
I think of the cash my father showed me
when I was young, when we moved off the farm
and the ponies had to be sold, even mine.
The money was so small, so inert.
I think he wanted me to hold it,
to accept the diploma of adulthood.
A letter came later, a photo — my pony
with her first foal, brown and white,
a baffled look on its face. Neither of them
will have lived this long; the money, too,
passed by now through a thousand hands.

Children Near the Water

Always there is much more happening than we can bear.
—TOMAS TRANSTRÖMER

When we wake in the warm tent
the children are already playing near the water.
Their sleeping bags are like empty wombs
with silky red lining.
From here they might be anyone's children,
or the earth's, one dark, one fair,
one girl, one boy.
It's been a long generation in my family
since any of us drowned.
Back then it was father's brother Joe,
the most beloved son
whose body washed ashore
on the sands of Lake Michigan.
How strange it is that water is both
life and death to us.
I think of my father as a boy
holding his mother all night long as she wept.

The face of the water
changes under the moving sun.
How stiff I am after sleeping on the ground.
No life left in last night's fire,
just soft gray ash and two soiled
marshmallow sticks.
Dew shines on a strand of spider silk
that binds a tall pine to the earth
like a guy wire. I think I know
what it must have felt like
to be the spider,
dangling in a lake breeze on the fragile
filament drawn from its own belly.
The children hardly notice as I join them.

They're so fresh,
like spruce buds in May.
Their feet are still round instead of long,
like smooth paws. How calm the water is today,
just the smallest ripples
wandering at the whim of the wind,
as many going out as there are
coming in.

A Field of Barley

Wind passes over a field of barley.
Nothing could be more lyrical.
Why God favored Abel's burnt meat
I'll never understand.

Sometimes I imagine the hills of Nod
covered with barley, and Cain standing alone,
dark with sunburn, wondering
what more he must do to be forgiven.

Years ago I visited a blooming orchard
on the east slope of the mountains
watered by its own spring, and I thought
I'd surely found Eden.

At night we saw city lights glowing
far out in the plain,
but the dark rock rose behind the farm,
eternal and absolute.

Up there one could see tragedy
long before it arrived,
foreshadowed in the first act.
Dust swelled behind its four wheels.

Dread is our inheritance.
But what sprouts out of the earth
is our consolation, the good yellow grain,
heavy in our arms.

Checkers

Red was passion, black was strength.
Yet one checker always had gone missing,
a deserter discovered eventually
cowering under a chair cushion.
What was there to fear?
Only time would be killed.

I was one who never planned ahead,
who sent my infantry into any open field.
Under my command they aspired
merely to be captured,
jumped and hauled off, bearing the smiles
of the successfully defeated.

Who really wanted to be kinged?
To stagger under a crown
heavy as a headstone,
to wander the board without a court
or even the escort of a fool?
What was glory? I never understood the word.

Often some idle soul of a certain age
taught checkers to the young,
offering stratagems
continually overruled by blind luck.
Then came snacks and naps
and afterwards, the balance of the day.

So Like Her Father

A glorious young bamboo
Has sprung up
Overnight!
—ISSA

My daughter sits cross-legged
on the tabletop and reads to me
as I wash the floor on my hands and knees.
Through an open door we smell the first lilacs.

In autumn she will leave this house.
I will never say the words
I remember from my father:
"When you return it will be as a visitor."

Still there exists a natural order
less compromising than our love, or hers,
or the love I bear my parents.

I scrub with water mixed with tears
and the footprints come away.
"I'm sorry," I say, "I wasn't listening."
She takes a sip of tea and begins again.

The Hammer

Here is an instrument as blunt
and hardheaded as its employer.
What has it done? It has forced the nail
waist deep into the wood,
while the nail has spoiled its pleasure
by bending. Now the hammer must
remove the nail with its huge teeth,
curved like goat horns.
The hammer must undo what is half-done
and begin again with a new, willing nail,
a nail that seems guileless as it says, "I do."

Crude work is in the hammer's very nature.
No one wonders where it is to be grasped
with the whole hand. It's clearly designed
to strike, to crack a brown-haired coconut
or a marrow bone. It's a fist, only harder.
The hammer's simple tongue is easily acquired:
a few elementary ejaculations
and one is fluent.

Deep in autumn I sometimes hear
a distant, solitary hammer
drumming on shingles or a two-by-four
while falling leaves foreshadow
something whiter and more serious.
How soon our days end—
yet the manly hammer is the last to retire.
Its head grows cold, its eyesight poor.
Is that a nail, the shadow of a nail,
a thumbnail? We'll know in a moment.

Tag

You're no longer "he" or "she"
but "it," neutered by a shoulder tap.
Good friends see you and run away, laughing,
and you stand in the middle of the yard,
alone with the contagion of your fingertips.

Perhaps you are the goat upon whose head
the guilt of a whole culture is amassed.
Or this is your moment to conclude
that every man *is* an island.

You are cast out of the tribe, left to wander
the steppes, recounting your innocence
to legions of flies and worms.
Your only hope of redemption
is to doom another to the same fate.

And the dusk is full of the children's shrieks and cries
as they dart from place to place
like trout startled by a human shadow.

Late September

The leaves grow lighter and lighter,
yet they fall. As the woods thin,
a house becomes visible,
and a plume of smoke hand-feeding the wind.
There's no hurry if you don't care.
For thirty years nothing knew paint,
but the house still stands.
What is dust, that we should mark
if it fills our empty boots while we sleep?

Children love you at first the way a dog does.
But eventually they will reveal
the history of your offenses
in high voices that carry across the pond.
Day opens and closes like a camera shutter,
mechanically, with more haste than necessary.
The cat lays a chipmunk at the back step.
I think of its burrow, of all it hoarded,
and of nine consecutive lives without remorse.

New Snow

A layer of smooth new snow
is like a coat of fat on the earth.
But it's only water weight we've gained —
it's insulation — it protects the crocus bulbs,
white as ovaries. How can another storm matter
on land so very old? These are woods, not a park;
snow comes and goes without formalities.

The whole top of a pine snaps off,
but the tree lives on. Imagine a symphony
that circles back upon itself endlessly. Musicians
fail and are replaced. Instruments fail
and are replaced. New genius. New snow.
The winds, freshened by open water,
take up the melody.

It's good to see old tracks buried,
then make them again,
and yet again. We fell into this life without a plan,
the way snow pours out of a white sky,
taking its shape from everything it finds.
We'll leave it the way
snow disappears in one warm night,
into the earth and into the air.

Grown Children

The full moon wakes the eldest son
on his makeshift cot in the living room.
You can sleep when you're dead, it says.
It's making good time across the sky
in spite of the wind,
like a car driving all night to cross the plains
ahead of the snow.

The grown children have returned in time
to say good-bye to their mother.
It's like Thanksgiving or Christmas,
cars parked on the lawn,
the little house so full. Early and late
lights are on; they feel guilty sleeping
or smiling or eating, rummaging
through her kitchen, observing
her needless frugality, cheese wrapped
in the lining of cereal boxes,
the freezer burning her day-old breads.
Between hospital visits they rake and chop wood
and keep the bird feeder full.

Who feels it most?
Who puts the coffee on at 3 a.m.?
Soon there will be no parent to shield him.
The curtain will open
and he'll be standing at the picture window
where anyone or anything might see him,
his silhouette, holding his hot mug, waiting
for the inevitable celestial evidence
that day will come.

Heart Surgery

That day I sat astride the roof ridge
sorting cedar shingles and nailing them
in long rows, planting them, two nails each,
my hands sweating in their gloves.
Nearby the portable phone, silent and white,
napped through all this noise, like a good baby.
Or as if it were anesthetized
like my father, five hundred miles west,
whose afternoon was completely devoted
not to bridge or the Giants' game,
but to heart surgery,
to paying death a call, and coming away.

I moved across the roof as the sun
moved across the sky, and my apprehension
was as big as the house beneath me.
My job was to follow the blue chalk line,
east to west, carrying bundles of fragrant wood.
No one waited below, worried sick,
for word the house would live.
There was no hurry. It was November
and it never rains in Albuquerque in November.

Rush hour was beginning—I could see far off
where shining cars poured onto the freeway—
when the phone rang. Mother. It had gone well . . .
there were others to call . . . she'd glimpsed him
on the gurney as they returned him to his room,
"and I thought he was dead, he was so blue."
The sky all around me was blue,
but night would change that soon.
A cool wind rose from the valley, from the river,
and I shivered, looking west over the city,
toward Phoenix, beyond the mesa, across the desert.
I would see my father again.

Thanksgiving Day. I entered his room alone,
without husband or child, and took his hand.
Our hands were as alike as my left is to my right,
one a little larger, used to doing more.
The shades were drawn
but he showed me, in the dark,
where they'd parted his chest,
and it was a coarse, enormous, fresh scar,
like the first furrow on the virgin prairie.
It had been, he said, "tougher than I'd anticipated."

But his face was already
more alive than it had been for years,
the color back, the blood flowing
like a river undammed, whole and free
as it once was, flooding the brown valley
as it once did, and his brow was smooth
as he lay back against his pillow,
and said he was ready to see the children.

All Saints' Day

It happens that the world has run out of patience.
Sleet coats a smashed pumpkin,
and the wraith hanging in an immature maple

must be lowered, washed and dried, and spread
again across the child's bed.
A north wind strips the popple of its costume, and flagellates

its bare limbs. The hills wear coarse gray, for penance,
before they're cowled in white.
And all the candy energy abroad last night,

the candle flame that lit up a malicious grin,
the brass of car horns,
the pillowcases bulging with extorted chocolates —

All is surrendered. The soul is a cold cell in November,
with one supernal window
admitting a wan light accessible only to those

who have given up the ghost.

Christmas Fable

Each day we pour fresh water
into the Christmas tree's saucer.
It doesn't know it's dead — all this
care suddenly, these lights and jewels,
a tiara and a thousand earrings
after the modesty of the forest.

So the woodcutter's daughter marries the prince,
but this is hardly the end.
Wherever she walks she leaves a trail
of pine needles and the tack of sap.
Her voice is like restless water
below ice too thin to bear hunting dogs.

How can we tell if we are happy?
Beyond the window, pines sleep standing up,
like horses tied to posts
waiting since childhood.
We're too old now to go far,
but they're still waiting.

After Us

I don't know if we're in the beginning or in the final stage.
—TOMAS TRANSTRÖMER

Rain is falling through the roof.
And all that prospered under the sun,
the books that opened in the morning
and closed at night, and all day
turned their pages to the light;

the sketches of boats and strong forearms
and clever faces, and of fields
and barns, and of a bowl of eggs,
and lying across the piano
the silver stick of a flute; everything

invented and imagined,
everything whispered and sung,
all silenced by cold rain.

The sky is the color of gravestones.
The rain tastes like salt, and rises
in the streets like a ruinous tide.
We spoke of millions, of billions of years.
We talked and talked.

Then a drop of rain fell
into the sound hole of the guitar, another
onto the unmade bed. And after us,
the rain will cease or it will go on falling,
even upon itself.

Hartley Field

And place is always and only place
And what is actual is actual only for one time
And only for one place.
—T. S. ELIOT

The wind cooled as it crossed the open pond
and drove little waves toward us,
brisk, purposeful waves
that vanished at our feet, such energy
thwarted by so little elevation.
The wind was endless, seamless,
old as the earth.
      Insects came
to regard us with favor. I felt them alight,
felt their minute footfalls.
I was a challenge, an Everest—

And you, whom I have heard breathe all night,
sigh through the water of sleep
with vestigial gills—

A pair of dragonflies drifted past us, silent,
while higher up two bullet-shaped jets
dragged their roars behind them
on unbreakable chains. It seemed a pity
we'd given up the sky to them, but I understand so little.
Perhaps it was necessary.

All our years together—
and not just together. Surely by now
we have the same blood type, the same myopia.
Sometimes I think we're the same sex,
the one in the middle of man and woman,
born of both as every child is.

The waves came to us, one each heartbeat,
and lay themselves at our feet.
The swelling goes down.
The fever cools.
There, where the Hartleys
grew lettuce eighty years ago,
bear and beaver, fox and partridge
den and nest and hunt
and are hunted. I wish I had the means
to give all the north back to itself, to let the pines
rise in the hayfield and the lilacs go wild.
But then where would we live?

I wanted that hour with you all winter—
I thought of it while I worked,
before I slept and when I woke,
a time when the tangled would straighten,
when contrition would become benediction:
the positive hour, shining like mica.
At last the wind brought it to us across the pond,
then took it up again, every last minute.

Selections from *On Speaking Terms*

First Snow

There were snows before I can remember,
famous snows that buried sheep alive,
Florida snows settling like pollen into orange blossoms,
and the first snow, a blizzard
drifting against the locked gate of Eden.

Afterward it was Eve who made
the first snowman, her second sin, and she laughed
as she rolled up the wet white carpet
and lifted the wee head into place.
"And God causeth the sun to melt her labors,
for He was a jealous God."

This time of year we count our summer blessings:
a series of disasters that passed south of us.
We walk the trails we'll soon be skiing;
you take my hand and tuck the knot they make
into your coat pocket. Each breath
is a little cloud capable of a single snowflake.

Monopoly

We used to play, long before we bought real houses.
A roll of the dice could send a girl to jail.
The money was pink, blue, gold, as well as green,
and we could own a whole railroad
or speculate in hotels where others dreaded staying:
the cost was extortionary.

At last one person would own everything,
every teaspoon in the dining car, every spike
driven into the planks by immigrants,
every crooked mayor.
But then, with only the clothes on our backs,
we ran outside, laughing.

Nothing

There are twelve hours in the day, and above fifty in the night.
—MARIE DE RABUTIN-CHANTAL

Nothing knew the time as she did,
but that was all she knew.
She stood at the window and watched
as snow clouds stole past like heavy-laden thieves
through a sky where nothing could hide
or be hidden,
where light steps accumulated through the hours
to vanish later in the sun.
She looked in on the sleeping children
and found them grown,
their heads and feet leagues apart,
their comforters thrown off
in their wild thrashing rest.
For each light that died, two lit up,
yet darkness endured.
So much labor led nowhere. So many words
led only to silence.
Nothing could be done at such an hour
but even that was more than she could do.

Tracks in the Snow

How was it I did not see that lofty sky before?
And how happy I am to have found it at last.
—LEO TOLSTOY

He lived in the house closest to the cemetery
and after a fresh snow
he liked to ski among the headstones.
New graves had an incline and a downward slope
that was gently exhilarating.
If people cared they never said so,
and his tracks were plainly legible,
a practiced signature
leading to and from his door.
He was as honest as the snow.

Old graves had settled and grown flatter
though he could still feel them under his skis.
Some years the snow rose until
even the headstones were buried.
Then the quiet intensified, and he could forget
it was a graveyard
but for those rare occasions when, midstride,
he stabbed his pole into the snow
and struck granite.

Rarely, but sometimes,
he fell: a lapse in concentration,
and then he thought,
"That's all it takes," and lying there,
"This is how it will be."
His skis formed an X at his feet
and the heart he seldom consulted
made itself known to him,
throbbing urgently in his ears:
Get up, get up, get up, get up.

The Accordion

for Hannah

It was the one tangible you brought home
from the city, an armful of instrument,
bellows and keys and buttons and a smell
of antique lubrication, and a sound that poured
undiminished through solid walls.
You sat in your chair with its straps around your shoulders
teaching yourself to play,
determined to do different things differently
in the tradition of your people,
mixed breeds from a dozen lands.
You sat as at a dance
with your partner on your lap, but it was also
a baby you were coaxing to speak.
I carried you that same way long ago,
your infant head under my chin, your chest against my chest,
my arms around you, my little marsupial.
I have photos of us like that: mother and child.
And more . . . I can feel it physically . . . my arms still ache . . .
it's like phantom pain after an amputation,
phantoms being real.
        You left it here with us,
the accordion, debating
whether to sell it, or to indulge yourself
by retaining such a large artifact, as it troubled no one
tucked back in your closet
in its battered, leather-covered case,
though neither was it useful.

Except it came to us at such a time:
you sat alone with it for hours
before your open curtains,
the music book awash in winter light,
hesitations, repetitions, small masteries,
and beyond you
snow passed through the sieve of the pine boughs
with the delicacy of grace notes.

Scrabble

I hoped to find solace in my letters,
perhaps even love,
a lover, or simply lovely.
I'm too old, too nervous for this endeavor.

Where are the words when it's my turn
to ask an honest question of the president?
My adversaries stare.
If only I could compose myself!

I need a *t* to give me time —
a *p* and I'd have help.
It's the story of my life,
rearranging assets and coming up shor.

At last I settle on an *s* that I can add
to something someone else has said,
making, of just one,
an infinite number of mistakes.

Directions

First you'll come to the end of the freeway.
Then it's not so much north on Woodland Avenue
as it is a feeling that the pines are taller and weigh more,
and the road, you'll notice,
is older with faded lines and unmown shoulders.
You'll see a cemetery on your right
and another later on your left.
Sobered, drive on.
    Drive on for miles
if the fields are full of hawkweed and daisies.
Sometimes a spotted horse
will gallop along the fence. Sometimes you'll see
a hawk circling, sometimes a vulture.
You'll cross the river many times
over smaller and smaller bridges.
You'll know when you're close;
people always say they have a sudden sensation
that the horizon, which was always far ahead,
is now directly behind them.
At this point you may want to park
and proceed on foot, or even
on your knees.

Lipstick

She leaned over the sink,
her weight on her toes,
and applied lipstick
in quick certain strokes
the way a man signs
his hundredth autograph
of the morning.
She tested a convictionless smile
as the lipstick retracted
like a red eel.
All day she left her mark
on everything she kissed,
even the air,
like intoxicating news
whispered from ear to ear:
He left it all to me.

Everything Free

The lake and sky were quarreling along the horizon:
late September. Whose fault was that?
The birches unburdened themselves
of the thinnest leaves in memory.

Where an old man had lived alone in quiet squalor
the yard was filled with boxes
and a sign: everything free.
He'd finally done as he'd promised;

he'd gone to Arizona to pan for gold.
People milled about, curious and disgusted,
and when every box had been overturned,
the shredded, chipped, tarnished, water-soaked, and smelly

goods determined to be irredeemable,
someone finally called the police.
The supply of clouds was inexhaustible, and the lake
had the sheen of titanium:

these were our riches.
There were gentler places to be poor.
People said he lived as he did because he was lazy
or lonely, but I believe

we all end up with what we really want.
Look around. You wanted this.
And I wanted one thing to remember him by
and took the sign.

Fishing on Isabella Lake

The lake was big enough to have islands,
a sign of wealth . . . my islands . . .
We saw a campsite on the largest
as we paddled by. No one there yet.
It was no particular day.
It was just day.

Once you could get far enough away,
but now you carry money with you even here.
The portage smelled like dust
and fish guts — a little altar on a stone,
a pile of viscera and heads, shining with prompt flies:
someone cleaned a few small walleyes.
Don't be sorry — they felt nothing.

Nothing you would recognize anyway,
though you've jabbed your fingers on lures,
and you've swum naked in a lake
without your glasses,
and your breathing has been labored,
your eyes stung by the sun.
At your most vulnerable moment
something rose in the periphery,
dangerous and indistinct, a rough underwater boulder
big enough to dump a canoe into the whitecaps
before you could even think a warning.

Save what you can, quickly —
but that gets harder and harder.
The lakes are low, drought and record heat,
southern summers creeping north
trailing their poisonous snakes
into Minnesota, a no-fault state
where we blame everyone, or no one.

I lost a fish at the canoe
without even seeing it.
My lure, suddenly free, leapt back at me.
I knew the fish was big
by the quality of its panic,
the line it drew against the drag.
I hated to lose it — I swore like a man.
One moment I looked into the lake
and it seemed full; the next moment, empty.

We smelled bear on the portage
but saw only an early star
burning through the jack pines — *Ursa Absentia*.
Not a star, but a planet with an accusatory stare.
We had the sun in common and little else.
Ours was the Goldilocks orbit,
not too hot, not too cold.
A day on the water
and all we could think of was sleep,
sleep and the lost fish.
We take things; we leave things behind —
and the sum of all this is zero,
or rather, one more day.

Garlic

A head of garlic swells
like a hobo's bundle. Pried open,
it's equally pungent.
Fresh garlic is good for you
if you crave solitude
and the open road.
Once I wrote a word
on the delicate paper I tore
from a garlic clove, a whimsy
that came out of my pores.
The word is gone, not forgotten,
like the man I lived with then.
Sometimes moderation is
not an option.
He's always in your bed;
he's never in your bed.
Garlic is or isn't in a dish
or sprouting
on the sunny windowsill,
an inch of green ambition
and a stirring
in the severed roots.

Rags

I dust with a sleeve I loved
to look at on my arm.
Blue is gray now, like a patch
of sky filthy with clouds.
Why is piano dust always so gray?
Something about sound waves
and decay
that science could explain.

I didn't need a scissors
the cotton was so rotted
by sun and sweat, the salt I made,
the sticky seawater. I was glad
to actually wear something out,
to have seen one thing
completely through,
even though I'd miss
being the person who wore it.

Lady

When I was young and lived on a farm
all our dogs were called "Lady"
even if they proved to be gentlemen.
We took in strays,
drop-offs that trotted across our fields
after town cars sped away.
Perhaps a child had turned to stare
through the back window. Freedom.
Like the end of a second marriage.
At least the dogs had a chance in the country;
it wasn't the pound.
The last Lady before we left the farm
was too shy to eat
while anyone watched.
She had low self-esteem perhaps,
but enormous litters, eight and nine and ten
not counting the doomed runts.
The neighbor's roaming collie
was the father; once I saw him (as I thought)
hurting her and I struck him with a shovel.
Well. He ran off the moment he could, of course.
Freedom. She looked up at me
with simple, fathomless eyes
and licked my dirty hand.
It wasn't thanks; it was acquiescence.
I think she was a Buddhist;
she bent in every wind, while her roots
went deeper and deeper.
When we left the farm we had to give her
to neighbors, the Tremls,
Joe, Jim, Judy, John, and Jenny.

Confessional Poem

I never told him anything
he didn't expect—
the white lies of a small girl,
a week's accumulations
related in halting, mouselike whispers.
He blessed me anyway
and gave me my penance
and bade me go in peace.
Perhaps the next penitent
would offer him what he came for,
a great, meaty, mortal sin like adultery
described in gorgeous language,
words that lit up the confessional
like a flashlight in a closet:
a silk cuff missing its button,
sheer stockings coiled on the floor,
shoes with heels like wineglass stems—
the hypnotic black-and-white images of film noir,
wherein all eyes followed a bad star
with uncontrollable longing.

Walking Distance

for Stanley Dentinger (1922–2004)

Walking distance used to be much farther,
miles and miles.

Your grandfather, as a young man
with a wife and new baby son,

walked to and from
his job, which was in the next town.

That was Iowa, 1946,
and it was not a hardship

but "an opportunity," which is youth speaking,
and also a particular man

of German descent, walking on good legs
on white gravel roads,

smoking cigarettes which were cheap
though not free as they'd been

during the war. Tobacco
burned toward his fingers, but never

reached them. The fire was small and personal,
almost intimate, glowing bright

when he put the cigarette to his lips
and breathed through it.

So many cigarettes before bombing runs
and none had been his last,

a great surprise. Sometimes he passed
a farmer burning field grass in the spring,

the smoldering line advancing toward the fence.
He had to know what he was doing,

so near the barn. You had to be close
to see the way

blades of dry grass passed the flame along
at a truly individual level,

very close to see how delicious a meal
the field was to the fire

on a damp, calm, almost English morning
ideal for walking.

The Splits

The world of my youth was divided
into girls who could and girls who couldn't
slide casually to the floor,
one leg aft and one fore, while their faces
retained a sprightly cheer.
All summer, all year
they stretched the critical tendons,
descending in increments
the way the willful enter a frigid lake,
their arms folded across their chests,
their backs burning in the sun
as their legs numb.
Yet the splits seemed less a skill
than a gift of birth: Churchillian pluck
combined with a stroke of luck
like a pretty face with a strong chin.
One felt that even as babies
some girls were predispositioned.

Buttercups

Corot's floating blooms (the tip of his brush
touches the canvas) a drop of cream
suspended over deep woodland green
(the scent of sun-warmed oils)
daisies, too, and something blue and tall, a harebell
(the palette crowded like a plaza)
with stems like wires that carry light
(the white sap that beads
when the weed is cut) up from the earth

(how anything wild can remain so clean)
an afternoon that is the lifetime of a blossom
(a bee asking to be painted, a commission!)
the buttercup shining as though varnished
(clouds slowing as the wind falls)
or waxed, even in the shade
(as though each sensation could be expressed
as a distinct tint) even in the lapel of a cotton smock.

Closest to the Sky

for Casey

I still feel like I'm trespassing
when I climb the attic stairs to your old room,
in all the house the place closest to the sky.
Signs of your former occupation:
mostly software — inessential shirts and socks —
and silver discs with whole worlds
collapsed into them,
worlds you conquered and tired of.
You left a tin of pennies on your dresser;
a guitar pick on the floor,
a blue triangle with softened points
and, if I had the dust and brushes,
your fingerprints.

These days your bed is never disturbed.
Here you lay for many weeks
healing after the accident. Perhaps that's why
both you and I avoid this place now.
Out the window an ancient spruce so near,
little more than arm's length: I can see every needle,
dull in the winter, sober green-gray,
a peaceful color
that never tries to cheer us falsely.
You used to complain about the crows
that woke you at daybreak
when they landed on the roof, a whole flock
shuffling overhead, cawing hard, calling for you.
Often I heard you swear at them out the window.
Now you're gone, but the crows only know
that no one here is angry anymore.

Comb

This comb has been here since my son left home.
When I run my thumb across its teeth
it makes a rough hum.
Stamped in gold are these words:
GENUINE ACE HARD RUBBER.
That's not much to go on, and really,
I don't care whence it came,
what wind blew it in. What concerns me
is how long I should keep it,
whether he might ever need it, miss it,
whether he has any memory of its parting
his hair on one side, then the other,
as he stood exactly here
before the mirror in the morning light
untangling the night.

Umbrella

When I push your button
you fly off the handle,
old skin and bones,
black bat wing.

We're alike, you and I.
Both of us
resemble my mother,
so fierce in her advocacy

on behalf of
the most vulnerable child
who'll catch his death
in this tempest.

Such a headwind!
Sometimes it requires
all my strength
just to end a line.

But when the wind is at
my back, we're likely
to get carried away, and say
something we can never retract,

something saturated from the ribs
down, an old stony
word like *ruin*. You're what roof
I have, frail thing,

you're my argument
against the whole sky.
You're the fundamental difference
between wet and dry.

Picture Yourself

. . . off the Gunflint Trail

A few ripples on the lake
folding themselves over like anonymous notes.
An idle day. Time slows here, as they say
it does in space; the minutes elongated,
lying in a long row in the sun,
stretching out, softening.
You ate your sandwich on the rocks
while your canoe waited like a dog on a leash:
it has all the fidelity (you were thinking),
all the eagerness of a spaniel.
It was company.

After dozens of failures
you finally remembered the camera.
You mounted it on a tripod of boulders
and composed the scene around
a missing man: you'd have ten seconds
to scramble into place
and turn back
before the shutter took its tiny bite.
This was exposure number twenty-three
on the mystery roll installed seasons ago
at Christmas (always, if nothing else, Christmas).
The camera saw what you saw
but it remembered.

Yet it felt nothing.
Only you knew the truth: not what you've done
but what you've felt
and wanted. Not what you've saved, either,

through years of supposed self-denial,
but all you've spent, and where,
such as here, a day alone on the water
revising your epitaph.

Was it vanity to arrange
the wilderness as your backdrop,
to motion the tamarack
a little to the left?
The woods answer only to the sun and wind.
Cedars lined the far shore with their roots
well below waterline, cedars with their burden
of near invincibility.

The color wouldn't be right. It never is.
One day you'd hold the photo and try to explain
how green it was that day,
how the quiet seemed to build to a crescendo,
the inertia to a climax.
How you wondered at your heart
beating past such a moment.

You adjusted the camera, worried about the battery:
old and bad, no doubt.
Perhaps it wouldn't matter
because the available light . . .
and here you paused, looking up . . .
Not a cloud. How often does this happen?

The Death of My Father

He died at different times in different places.
In Wales he died tomorrow,
which doesn't mean his death was preventable.
It had been coming for years,
crossing the ocean, the desert, pausing often,
moving like water or wind,
here turned aside by a stone,
then hurried where the way was clear.

Once I lay on my back in the grass and watched
as cloud after cloud moved east
and disintegrated. The mystery now
is not where they went, but how
I could ever have been so idle.

Funerals are all the same.
I saw him cry at his mother's wake
when I was young enough to be
picked up, lofted into someone's arms.
He, a man, cried that day,
but people smiled, too. You think now
you want to be remembered,
but the dead don't care.
My grandmother's face said that.

Indifference is a great relief, after a lifetime
of mothering one's many worries,
trying not to play favorites.

I wasn't present when he died.
I feel that keenly, that I should have
had a share. I was spared
unfairly. I was not fed
the bitter broth and the hard bread.

What time did it happen
exactly? What was I doing at that exact moment?
What can I do now?

But the moment is never exact.
One dies over years — yes, there is a first breath
and a last, yet consider a cut tulip
upright in a vase, closing as the day ends,
then turning toward the morning window, opening again.
One day I touch a petal and it falls off.
Even so the balding stem takes
another sip of water.

My mother held the phone to his ear
so each middle-aged child could say a distant good-bye,
and she searched his face for a sign.
Perhaps. No one knows what he heard
or if a phone was essential to it.
The longing to believe is more enduring
than any truth — truth is so perishable.
I once was found, but now I'm lost.
I could see, but now I'm blind.

A Sighting

The gray owl had seen us and had fled
but not far. We followed noiselessly,
driving him from pine to pine:
I will not let thee go except thou bless me.

He flew as though it gave him no pleasure,
forcing himself from the bough,
falling until his wings caught him:
they had to stroke hard, like heavy oars.

He must have just eaten
something that had, itself, just eaten.
Finally he crossed the swamp and vanished
as into a new day, hours before us,

and we stood near the chest-high reeds,
our feet sinking, and felt
we'd been dropped suddenly from midair
back into our lives.

Green Tent

Erect, the green tent is a gable,
the attic of the earth.
We enter on hands and knees,
by means of a long zipper
delicately undone.
Inside we're still outside,
still vulnerable
to a leaning pine or a bear
rummaging through the pantry.
The walls are green drapes;
they're a green balloon
we filled by sighing.
It's home, though, a studio apartment
you invited me to
where the only place to sit
is the bed.

Pumpkin

None is so poor that he need sit on a pumpkin.
—HENRY DAVID THOREAU

To write as a field grows pumpkins,
to scribble page after page with an orange crayon,
to lose teeth and still smile,
to survive a frost that blackened acres,
to wake after surgery.

To live without rotting from within,
to ignore imperfections of the skin,
to be heavy, and still be chosen,
to please a strict vegetarian,
to end the day full of light.

A Random Gust from the North

RUNOFF

Another hottest summer ever.
Storms with the violence of a broken atom.
Storms that drove the boats in
and smashed them in their slips. Power out for days,
so we lived by the sky, like any animal.
Runoff turned the bay red
as from some ancient slaughter—
the smelt runs, perhaps, every spring of your youth
when fish crowded the river mouths
so thickly you could reach down with only your hands
and take all you wanted
and people did. In the evening
we knelt on the boulders by the big lake
and washed our forearms
in the surges that rose against the stone,
and the water we loved was cold enough to kill us.

SUNFISH

His ribs were thick as barrel staves,
his heart full of chambers such as waves
carve out of granite,
smooth caverns accessible only by boat.
His toes were like mushrooms,
misshapen by the sealed can of a boot.
They had the look of fish bait
as indeed they were
when as a child he sat on the weathered dock,
the soft gray boards, his feet
dangling in the lake, and sunfish
nibbled his toes. Sunnies.
What was death, but sunlight on the water?

Now he set herring nets on summer mornings
while the village slept. His boat was unnamed,
a workboat among the pleasure craft
in the marina. Nothing polished,
no illusions, no vanity.
He left the harbor on an open palm
held out to the lake and sky.
He was an offering.
Good days he filled the boat with thrashing fish
drowning in oxygen. It was the same fish
over and over, like page after page
to the illiterate.
This man with a kind disposition
sold his catch, and thus he lived.
"North," he said, and the word itself
spoke, offering hardship and darkness and solitude,
and he trembled like a compass needle.

SOUTH WIND

Sometimes he caught a fish that had cancer.
A south wind carried the stench of the paper mill.
South. A single city sixty miles across.
Thousands of cars on the freeway,
all sizes and sorts, like fish
forced together by low water
or by a net. The air he was obliged to breathe,
air that had passed through
smokestacks and motors and ducts and countless
living lungs before his and after,
air that had a history,
that had come to the city years ago
blown in from the alfalfa fields
to enter a copse of mirrored towers
now seen, now lost in the sky,

to swirl in a courtyard
rising and falling through the hours
without passion or purpose
but with exhilarating ease.
Flocks of ravens gathered in the dirty park,
shining like the jewelry of the Aztecs
polished by slaves.
Heat waves rose from the grid, a conflagration
that seared the silver bellies of the jets.
There were highways among the clouds
or else the sky was but another blue sea
and planes were passenger ships,
as birds were fish,
as wind was a current.
Why lament? So goes the wind. South.
Here is the puncture
where poison entered the body.

A SMALL VESSEL IN THE SWELLS

He took up the rope
and drew the boat toward him like a pony.
It woke as he stepped into it
and settled obediently under his weight.
Then the canter of a small vessel in the swells,
the bow high, power
from the churning hindquarters.
He went out against the will of the lake.
The water red as the sunrise:
he was crossing the sky.
Later it would be rough,
perhaps dangerous,
the warning repeated every few seconds
until it goes unheeded.
Where does a wave begin?

Before memory,
in the quick pulse of a mother's blood
pouring into the bay of the womb.
Impossible to say whether the water
speaks from within or without.
Ashore again, he felt the earth
rock on its fulcrum; standing on shore
he felt land-sick, drained, short of breath.

THE NORTH SHORE

A cabin so small it is like a woodpecker hole
smelling of fresh pine pitch.
Like a new-made pauper's coffin.
Calm today. One feels the depth of the lake,
the weight of an iron anchor
falling through the fathoms.
Here or there a surface disturbance,
a boat wake, a few gulls bickering over fish offal,
then a random gust from the north.
The lake wrinkles the way a horse,
dozing in the shade, jerks its skin
where a fly lands.
Waves come to shore backward, blindly,
like a horse backing into wagon traces
with a sack over its head.
If a horse knew its strength
it could never be tamed.

A LAST READING

The north pole. Instruments alone confirm it.
And what if the instruments disagree?
Can there be such an absolute arrival?
Or does realization come later,
far too late for the champagne?
And what of ambition?

Surely it precedes a man by months, years,
and has already published its memoirs.
Here one senses the attention
of every compass in the world
pointing like a crowd of fingers
toward a tightrope stretched between
clouds. A lone figure looks everywhere
but down. So much light,
light to spare, light to spread on the ice like salt.
The pole afloat; we are neither first
nor last, though perhaps nearer the last.
We need no instruments.
The equatorial vertigo subsides;
the heat of exertion dissipates.
We have no fear of falling.
We can never be lost.

Musical Chairs

The music, quavering and faint,
had somehow kept order among us.
But when it stopped
everyone rushed toward the lifeboats
where seats were scandalously insufficient.

Why had our parents given birth to so many of us?
They expected us to share, perhaps,
or they couldn't imagine science failing in the end,
unsinkable science, the laboratory of miracles
where mice lived as quietly as they could.

Perhaps the sea would take us all finally,
perhaps the earth. Meanwhile
a tranquilizing waltz began
and we left the safety of our seats. The line of us,
which was really a circle, began to inch forward.

A Parting

after Wang Wei

Mother:

> We have to say good-bye again so soon.
> Another seam torn open, another hole in the pocket
> discovered too late.
> You're going where the snow falls
> as rain; you're leaving
> through the gate that opened in a wall of clouds:
> go quickly.
> Call me every night unless you're happy.
> Then I can tell myself
> that all the silent evenings
> are what I want.

Son:

> You've done all you can — be satisfied.
> More and my thanks would be
> like tea steeped too long,
> tinged with bitterness.
> The bear is dreaming somewhere under the snow
> but I can't sleep for thinking of the road
> that changes color: gray here, yellow in the south.
> Don't worry. I'll greet the wild goose for you,
> the one you fed all summer
> in the reeds by the wide river.

Pecans

The travelers brought us pecans from Las Cruces
and I saw again the place I lived so long,
where the Rio Grande flows wide and shallow.
I saw my father with his eyes closed,
basking in the early sun,
sipping a cup of strong black coffee.
I saw my mother pacing the dry yard, planning
the pear and apple trees she'd grown up north
that suffered so during desert summers.
I stood again at the kitchen sink, looking out,
my hands idle in the dishwater,
and watched a vagrant stoop in the back alley
to fill his pockets with fallen pecans.
He was passing through, heading for the coast,
guided by instinct like waterfowl.
Why we must go we can't say.
Some blame the heavens, the restless stars,
some the earth, spinning under our feet
like a ball under an acrobat.

In the palm pecans resemble a clutch of wild eggs,
brown and oblong, full of blueprints.
The trees themselves were the pride of the yard;
their green shelter and the scent of their shade
reminded Mother of her Wisconsin.
When we walked beneath them in late fall
we stepped on pecans, and they cracked
against the dry earth. Sometimes we all pitched in
to pick them up, all the sisters and brothers,
working under threat of punishment, or cajoled with bribes.
In those days we owned a black border collie
that ran away every night
with every intention of coming home,
though one night she finally didn't.

I wonder at those
who stay in the same place their whole lives;
I wonder where I'll die.
At some point we just want what's easiest.

Pecans are not native to Las Cruces;
they need far more rain than falls in the desert.
But water flows all summer from the river,
diverted through long muddy ditches,
and the trough of the valley
fills with greenery and bees. A place is both itself
and what we make of it, as we are ourselves
and what a place makes of us.
No Waneks at all are left in that town.

The travelers brought pecans, coarse and rustic,
the husk still attached to one or two,
here a bark fragment, a blade of blond grass.
I was glad to see them.
Only one pecan in perhaps a million sends out roots,
a sturdy green shoot,
and by some accidental or deliberate circumstance
becomes a tree that blooms and bears
year after year in the same soil.
The rest of the pecans are organized and eaten.
If this is sad, tell me what is not sad.

Old Snow

Thaws have taken their toll,
and once rain fell across the white hills.
The snow is half ice now,
granulated and industrial, and the men
in the yard have lost their coal teeth
and are hollow-eyed and helpless.
They've been loyal to the picket line
all winter, watching scabs come and go.

Old snow has layers like a canyon wall,
a season precisely recorded,
what died when: fossilized crab apples
shaken loose by a historic wind,
feathers from a lost wren.
Soon the hardest snow will form
a black mirror on the road, and the luck
of this tough old town will turn.

Pickles

I don't need to say what they look like, do I?
Surely everyone who's bitten the end
off a stiff little gherkin
has had the same unwholesome thought.

The jars are nearly always short and stout
though pickles are not caloric.
With their broken dill and sunken detritus
the jars remind me of long-neglected aquariums;

and in fact we have some very old pickles
inhabiting a swampy corner of the fridge, passed over
time and again by a doubtful hand.

The pickles may be growing legs by now
and croaking all night
in the cold spring of the icebox, silenced
by the slightest movement of the door.

Coloring Book

Each picture is heartbreakingly banal,
a kitten and a ball of yarn,
a dog and bone.
The paper is cheap, easily torn.
A coloring book's authority is derived
from its heavy black lines
as unalterable as the Ten Commandments
within which minor decisions are possible:
the dog black and white,
the kitten gray.
Under the picture we find a few words,
a caption, perhaps a narrative,
a psalm or sermon.
But nowhere do we discover
a blank page where we might justify
the careless way we scribbled
when we were tired and sad
and could bear no more.

Blue Ink

Blue ink is friendlier than black,
more feminine. You can sign the papers
and still believe
it's not quite final.

You can conjecture in blue ink,
and write a check for more than you have.
People will understand.

Some days the lake is blue enough
to be bottled, or injected
directly into a pen,

though as the words dry
they disappear, letter by letter,
sparing you
serious embarrassment.

Six Months After My Father's Death

It was Mother on the phone, and she sounded
well, finally out of his misery.

Her breathing was good, her lungs
clear, after the near suffocation

of his last year. He hadn't meant to hurt her.
Drowning people will do anything for air.

"Do you still hear his whistle?" I asked,
and she said, "Sometimes it

wakes me in the morning, yes."
It had hung, silver and serene, near his hand

and in her last dream.
Or was it the mockingbird she heard

that took up the summons he had mastered?
What with her nearly deaf and him so feeble

some last calls surely went unanswered
and some answers came faithfully

in response to nothing
more than a gray bird perched

at the top of a lemon tree,
pleading for help.

Honey

Luxury itself, thick as a Persian carpet,
honey fills the jar
with the concentrated sweetness
of countless thefts,
the blossoms bereft, the hive destitute.

Though my debts are heavy
honey would pay them all.
Honey heals, honey mends.
A spoon takes more than it can hold
without reproach. A knife plunges deep,
but does no injury.

Honey moves with intense deliberation.
Between one drop and the next
forty lean years pass in a distant desert.
What one generation labored for
another receives,
and yet another gives thanks.

Leftovers

After you have read all you possibly can
there may be a few lines left.
Please don't feel obligated!
They're cold by now
as conclusions often are.
Hard, too, like beef fat that
whitens at the foot of a roast.
Some can make another meal of leftovers
and often read past midnight
drinking the last wine
directly out of the bottle.
"Happily ever after" is for those
who never seem to tire of sweets.
And you: you're already going home,
leaving me with this mess,
wrinkled napkins, bones and crusts
and onions teased out of the salad.
If only I had a pig to fatten
on last words.

Ice Out

The south wind discovers a loose thread
and winter begins to unravel.
The first black and blue butterfly
materializes. The second.
They find each other.

The snow fort is in ruins.
Stacks of ammunition
have melted into the grass.
A floatplane with stiff wings
banks over the pines, turning north;
an eagle, too, searches for open water.

Open water. A window to the bottom.
Sometimes the water is so clear
that it hardly exists
except as a change in viscosity.
The island has its moat again,
the moon its mirror.

New Poems

PART ONE

*. . . in which we work our way
to the center, song by song*

Garter Snake

But the serpent said to the woman, "You will not die."
—GENESIS 3.4

If you were whole and willing
I'd invite you under my skirt
to hold up my stocking,
little snake, silk muscled and elastic.

But you're timid, and you've lost
your tail tip: a mishap
in a cool August foreshadow,
or unluck among hawks.

I'm glad you aren't your brother.
I found him, flat and empty,
crossing the road, pressed smooth
by one tread after another.

Charming! Your serious eyes
and quick pink tongue, your
swimmy gestures toward the garden,
your *liquefaction*.

I'm right behind you, darling,
though we're both cautious
and curious. All these years on earth,
yet I still have a thousand questions.

Pollen

The neighbor's bees, his chattel,
are healthy again, and back they've come
to work in my garden.

What shelter's more felicitous than
a squash blossom? The bees are busy, yes,
but do they know enough to call that happiness?

Living dust clings to their legs
and wings. Six male flowers tremble
for every pregnant bloom,

and to touch them is a terrible intimacy.
How can bees be property?
How can a garden?

Small white houses in an orchard:
A good life, near the children,
near the graves.

Rival Gardens

Some made a bargain with the Devil
and boasted of their yields,
how tall, how many pounds,

even how hard it was to turn
the earth with a simple spade.
Some spun yarns about

woodchucks caught in the act,
then poisoned like King Gonzago
or trapped in the fancies of Master Poe.

Some buried well-rotted droppings,
then Jack's magic beans;
some kept Peter out of the carrot row.

My corn never brushed the heavens;
God and Satan left me alone.
My tomatoes were mediocre,

my lettuce bitter in the heat.
Still I counted every modest thing
twice, and called the world fair.

The Summerhouse

I wanted a wall to kneel before, planting hollyhocks.
Yes, a folly — more whimsy than work,
crooked if that's what it took. I wanted to be seven
for a day in a playhouse my father built,
though he was never that sort of man. I'd need
a hook for my hat and a hook for my jacket
on a tugboat sailing through the birches, pulling
(at a safe distance) the rest of the world.
It would be a blind, too, where we'd hide to watch
the black bear saunter down our apple-tree-trail,
and the fall buck scrape the velvet from his antlers
on anything handy, anything hard. I wanted
to paint clean pine boards in the autumn
with long brushstrokes, the way you run your hand
across a horse's back, from the withers to the rump.
If I closed my eyes and said, "There's no place
like home," where would the whirlwind take me?

Polygamy

Some men don't hate marriage,
or slavery for that matter.
Nor can they ever own enough land.

When I was a girl back on the farm
I surprised a wild tomcat in the hayloft.
He was eating a kitten,

its eyes still shut tight
like apple buds. The shutter clicked
as he looked at me, his expression fixed.

I still think he knew what he was doing,
though not why,
which makes him almost human,

or makes us almost feline.
I could hear the other kittens
mewing softly

somewhere in the hay,
deep in the hidden nest
established by our cat

when she felt them coming.
How many did he take, I wondered,
and how can I punish him?

The Neighbor's Pond

What I do is me: for that I came.

—GERARD MANLEY HOPKINS

A moose came to bathe
one rare hot first of June, wading in
belly deep, his winter coat half-shed,
his haunches patchy.
He scattered the ducks, and the heron
lifted off, each movement
sharp as scissors.
The moose seemed lost
in thought: it's summer
and I'm alone. Why?
He shook himself to dislodge
the wretched blackflies; but no,
they came right back. They required
blood, while he, big as he was,
lived on water lilies.
His hooves roiled the muddy bottom.
Whatever he touched, he broke.
After he splashed out
the pond required hours
to restore its serenity,
its post-moose-ness. A moose
barges into the blue-green world
as though he didn't belong
where he clearly does, as though
his whole life was one long riddle
and the answer was
backwards and upside down
in pieces on the water.

An Ordinary Crisis

I don't recall what final unfairness
made me pack to run away, whether it was
fall or spring. Either matched my haste.
Everything I needed fit into a pillowcase.

I had read about hobos, stuffed bandanas
on a stick, jackets lined with grass for warmth.
I knew what I was doing. My cousin
had taught me how to whistle.

I was crying, though; I remember that.
It's so much harder to cry now
unless I see someone dear overwhelmed,
especially a man. I suffer a diminished

capacity to drag a dirty pillowcase
through a ditch. At the border, staring toward
the railroad tracks, into the immensity,
my mother found me and ordered me back

to the house. A little relieved, I obeyed.
I've always come home, or
wanted to. I've always been easy to convince,
given the least kindness.

Mysterious Neighbors

Country people rise early
as their distant lights testify.
They don't hold water in common. Each house
has a personal source, like a bank account,
a stone vault. Some share eggs,
some share expertise,
and some won't even wave.
Last November I saw a woman down the road
walk out to her mailbox dressed in blaze orange
cap to boot, a cautious soul.
Bullets can't read her no trespassing sign.
Strange to think they're in the air
like lead bees with a fatal sting.
A walk for the mail elevates the heart rate.
Our neighbor across the road sits in his kitchen
with his rifle handy and the window open.
You never know when. Once
he shot a trophy with his barrel resting on the sill.
He's in his seventies, born here, joined the navy,
came back. Hard work never hurt a man
until suddenly he was another broken tool.
His silhouette against the dawn
droops as though drought stricken, each step
deliberate, down the driveway to his black mailbox,
prying it open. Checking a trap.

Catbird

The catbird fanned his tail in May
the way a man strums his half-tuned guitar,
string by string. Then he began to sing
his song of songs: borrowed notes,
phrases lifted from the public domain.
Thank no one. Pay no one.
Soon she came fluttering to the wire,
slender and gray.

In May you cut your winter-long hair outside,
silver trimmings on the wind.
The catbirds made their selection,
lining their tinseled nest.
Eggs appeared, a sensible two.

Just two. And the singing ceased
in favor of secrecy, stealthy
comings and goings in the honeysuckle hedge.
Why do we regard all this as instinct?
As opposed to what? Reason?
Why did we have children?
Because I suddenly wanted to.
That was our reason.

One day you came through the open summer door.
"Something terrible has happened."
You had found a half-fledged chick
drowned in the rain barrel
and pulled it out with a clothespin.
A few days later the other lay near the driveway,
its tiny beak swarming with ants.
That's business. That's capitalism.
And from the center of the hedge
the mother called to them all day,
and again all day, and again.

I listened as I pollinated squash blossoms
with a watercolor brush.
Where were the bees this year?
She sang in a minor key,
and I took it personally. Sometimes love
seems just another word for work.
But we can't let that stop us.

That same summer weddings came to pass,
and divorces. Homes stood empty.
The chances were never quite fifty-fifty.
But for scavengers the odds were better.

Root Words

for Joyce Sutphen

Tug a carrot out of the earth, an orange
tooth, and brush it right there in the garden.
Wash it in the rain barrel, the water
tinted gold like Listerine. Now it's clean,

a root with delicate roots of its own,
and greens like wild Irish hair gathered up
in your fingers, limp in the August heat.
Good work adds up: it's physically-logical.

We are happiest in context, our feet
bare again in the summer garden, where
seeds we tapped out in April have become
all we can talk about (except children).

We love the earth we came from, and the sky
we're lofted into, and (first and last) words.

Rain Collection

The oldest rain in the barrel
is snowmelt, light and clear as a bridal veil,
sullied only by an inch of late sleet.
Wedding weather can't be ordered, sadly,
though heaven knows we tried.
Of June's downpours many gallons remain,
sun warmed and alive with mosquito larvae.
So much fell, in fact, that we retained
nothing of July, but let the hawkweed
drink it all. Summer's
the vintage my grandmother loved.
Not long before she died
she asked my mother,
"Betty, could you do one thing?
Could you wash my hair in rainwater?"
August showers came unpinned,
yellow-silver, flowing over the stones.
To *husband* the estate,
to know what can be spared,
is commonly the province
of wives and daughters.
For often autumn rain will vanish
between falling and landing,
like a child bolting up
out of a nightmare.

Blue Flags

A vector field is complete if its flow curves exist for all time.
—R. W. SHARPE

High in the mountains
blue flags bloom along
the cold creek that crosses
a summer pasture
on the diagonal,
the longest vector,
infinite on both ends.

This iris is the wild blue
I've been lost in all my life.
The soft sabers of the leaves
bend away as I bare
its elegant stem. Should I?
Then the greens spring back,
on guard again.

Don't let me die until the blooms do.
Don't let me die until I see
this very blue in a newborn's eyes.
Don't let me die
while I'm still in love.
Yes, I could go on and on
nourishing the irises
with my ashes,
and they would take me up,
and repeat after me.

High in the mountains
blue flags bloom along
the dark creek that crosses
a summer pasture
on the diagonal,
the longest vector,
infinite on both ends.

"Golden Glow"

(Rudbeckia laciniata var. hortensia)
for Robyn Dentinger

She called it the outhouse flower:
eight feet tall that August,
eight feet deep into the air.
Goldfinches bloomed there,
wind-ruffled, the females
greener, the males ego-bright.
Persistent accidents, over time,
amend the constitution.
A late squall broke
the stems in two, gusty rain,
shouting from the pulpit.
Never trust an orator who grips
the podium with both hands.
Then off flew the goldfinches,
and summer followed
their wake of yellow petals.

Blackbirds at Dusk

We fell in love near blackbirds, a tree full.
Among bare November branches
the birds became its fruit.

We couldn't trust blackbirds not to tell.
A kiss, and they took flight
all at once, circling the bell tower
like a black scarf caught in a wheel.

The wheel never stopped. We can say that
about a few good things.
We could see spring—last and next—
on every dark wing.

First House

We bought a house made of mud and straw.
Thieves stole my sewing machine
and my turquoise ring.
They stole your music, and the needle
you lowered with one steady finger.
To lose these things. I learned.
We had a little girl
and I never let her out of my arms.

Summer nights we sat on a moon-striped
back porch. Later I hung out
laundry in the snow, glorious whites.
Clothespins clung to the wire,
a flock of house finches,
breasts to the sun. Like a needle
we rode the world as it spun,
working our way to the center,
song by song.

Last Star

Open the coming day to the table of contents.
The first chapter, "The Last Star," begins
"All the fawn's spots faded, except one."

It seemed the robin would never stop singing,
if singing's the word. More like
the scribbles of a child imitating cursive,
certain everything means something.

Does a mare remember being a foal
as she cares for her own, her first?
"Suddenly I found my neck
was long enough, and I could graze."
Afterward she forgot the taste of milk, but she
kept the white star shining on her forehead.

Perhaps this day holds such promise
you turn first to the last page, to be sure.
The one you love most must still be alive,
or you'll go no further.

PART TWO

. . . in which my mother
ponders, is any of it true?

Used Book

for Charles Baxter

I out-read the marginalia:
the last pencil tread
was a lone exclamation point
on page 73. A scenic overlook,
a historical marker. My mother
always pulls over to read and ponder:
is any of it true?
I turned west on a narrow
highway sketched on a paper napkin.
That road gave me to another,
equally lonely, and I made
good time, feeding the horses
gasoline. At last I saw mountains
like the blue base of a flame,
and I turned the page.
What I needed was a motel by dark
and a glass of any wine.
I grew anxious. Many years had passed
since I could, like a gypsy,
sleep wherever I found myself.
Then through the windshield glare
I saw a hitchhiker, even more desperate
than I was, his destination
scribbled on a cardboard sign.
My foot touched the brake,
then the gas again.

Ghost Town

People hate being wrong.
Once they galloped here
on lathered horses
sick with avarice, and slept
on their daily tailings,
and squeezed into the dark every morning.
They named their holes
Lucky something or something Luck.
Another rumor took them farther west
like a funnel of hornets.

Now someone's building
near the ghost town
on a scar he made, a red gash
across the foothills. Talk is
he's a gun dealer from Deming,
planning to hole up there
when the world ends
with his spirits and spoils
and big white Dodge Ram,
another Lone Ranger, but without
the crippling philanthropy.
He has all four aces in his pocket,
yes, but the jokers are wild.

When I Was a Boy

I wouldn't try your patience.
Not like a black lab with a tennis ball
that won't drop it, however much
he wants you to throw it again.

I would race to win, openly,
when I was a boy. I took after
my father then, and when I saw
a tossed butt in the gravel

still fuming, I picked it up
and raised it to my lips, like a man.
I knew precisely where
Wanek property ended, and I ordered

other children off our land
when it pleased me to do so.
I had a cap gun and rolls of tiny red
explosions to force-feed it.

I was not yet convinced
that when people died,
they stayed dead, because
when I was a boy

friends rose again from the field,
grass in their long hair, having grown
ten seconds older, ten seconds
closer to their other fates.

Audience

How kind people are!
How few in the crowd truly hope
the tightrope will break.

Rare's the man who'll shoot the Pope
or throw his shoe at a liar,
though joining in — that's natural.

An audience of St. Paul's sparrows
is easily bored, easily frightened.
One blasphemy and off they fly.

Even a polite dog will snore
through reprimands,
though he'll rouse to follow

the refreshments with a calculating eye.
But people, especially Minnesotans,
pull their sleeves over their watches

and want to find a way to like you.
If they can sit through winter's sermons,
they can sit through you.

John Q. Public

In line at the post office, again
at the library, he told me who he was.
Name, of course, which his father
had kindly given him, but most important
was his secret identity. How it feels to have one.

Tragic if he died with his research incomplete!
Some mornings he made no progress at all,
but sold a few books, ate a sandwich.

Afternoons he resumed his pursuit
of the perfect sponge, dense and damp
by nature. Without that,
one could clean nothing well.

"The mind," he tapped his temple.
Language is too crude a tool,
like a crowbar or sledgehammer
or a two-man crosscut saw.
"What I'm thinking!" he said.
"If only I could tell you!"
Gently, I took his hand off my arm.

A Collection of Near Misses

"It's almost good,"
she said to her companion
as she held it at arm's length
and squinted at it:
a landscape with cows.
She checked the price. Five dollars.
All the art at the Salvation Army
Thrift Store was on sale today.

The frame alone. And the colors
were hers, western blues
and eastern greens, the vivid
black-and-white Holsteins.
"What I don't like . . ."
her companion began, and then
the critic entered the deliberations.
"If it weren't a little ridiculous,
I wouldn't have it,"
said woman number one,

who took it to the cash
register before she could change
her mind. Out in the parking lot,
in the bright sun,
she knew she'd done the right thing.
Five dollars for all the longing
and self-doubt in her hands.
One cow had raised its square head
to look directly at her.

Adaptation

His surname was Johnson.
He was one of the thousand Garys
born that week in the fifties
when people had no ready term
for every minor variation
from the norm. People were not
crazy then, or they were.
He had a thin face,
placid as a Modigliani,
his skin the shade of lake fog,
his hair beach-sand tan.
He wore perma-press slacks
an inch too short, that matched
his beige zip-front jacket.
How to describe a man who took
such pains to be nondescript:
he was like a curious word that,
once you finally learn its meaning,
you see everywhere.

He read the paper at the library,
always yesterday's
so no one cared how long he took,
sitting in the corner behind the stacks
shaking the paper straight
as though in his living room chair.
He had opinions, my yes!
If anyone should ask.
Presumably he had a mother who
had stopped expecting him to give her
anything delightful to tell her friends.

He dined at art openings. Olives
and cheese cubes. Grapes, one by one.
Sometimes the table was lavish.
A little loaded plate
trembled in his long fingers.
But he did his part and stared
at the white walls bright with frames
and all the odd things people wore.

Plein Air

He wanted to say what he felt
while he still felt it
as he sat before the contours
of his longing. It was alive
with shadows and windy light:
long grass bowing over and over,
polite, even reverent,
and smooth, the way young lungs
fill and empty without oversight,
and sometimes a fall warbler
caught up in the instant
sailed by. *How will I die — how
can I?* he asked, his brush still wet.
*Will it come at a moment
of indecision? What color is it?
Must I agree?*
If so, he'd live forever
because he'd never agree, never!
The present, sun-charged,
rushed into his hand.

The Death of the Battery

A shell of light held our faces together,
a Caravaggio. Then the battery,
AA, the bright one, the safe investment,
began to die. An amber varnish
darkened the ancient canvas.

It wasn't the kind of battery
you could rest overnight, like a good horse,
and harness again at dawn.
It hadn't nine lives, like a mouser.
It brought nothing winged
back from the rough November marsh
to drop at your boot.
You couldn't praise it or punish it.

Still you wanted everything
the battery owed you.
You quickened as I slowed. You rose
as I sank, until finally I turned
to the dark window, where among
the summer birches flickered
the child-beckoning fireflies.

Girdle

In our teens we all bought girdles
with rubber knobs to hold up our stockings.
We wiggled into them, our "foundations."

So many things look absurd from a distance
that people still take seriously,
like whether there's a Heaven for pets.

What ever happened to my girdle?
One day I peeled it off for the last time
and all hell broke loose.

Parts per Million

A clear night, the winter stars
seated: the bolt tightens a half-turn,
the water's gone hard, the bear's in bed.
All's pure. The cold demands it.

A star for every wish we ever had
and many we have yet to make,
stars sharp enough to scratch glass,
bright enough to read by.

To feel lost — that's human, fear not.
So few parts per million. Two?
Two left standing in a white field
opposite the stars.

Mrs. God

Someone had to do the dirty work,
spading the garden, moving mountains,
keeping the darkness out of the light,
and she took every imperfection personally.

Mr. Big Ideas, sure,
but someone had to run the numbers.
Then talk about babies: he never imagined
so many.

That was part of his charm, of course,
his frank amazement at consequences.
The pretty songs he gave the finches:
those spoke to his

innocence, his ability to regard
every moment as fresh. "Let's give them
free will and see what happens,"
he said, ever the optimist.

Genesis, Cont.

Other days God seemed severe,
but he was always hardest on himself.
Curious, he watched Mrs. God,
the way she distanced herself
from disasters. Especially the ones
he himself unintentionally set in motion.

All God asked for was eternal work.
Luckily something was always broken.
A virus began to kill all its hosts,
or claws needed sharpening, and afterwards
he had to make them retractable.
Weather was a challenge,

finicky, like those old carburetors.
But gravity turned out perfectly:
hummingbirds could fly, but people
didn't float around, and two legs worked fine.
Mrs. God's radiant smile, yes, he gave that
to the sun, and all the stars, and then to Eve.

Day of Rest

The good Lord had primer on his hands,
but paint could wait till Monday,
Mrs. God assured him, seeing how tired he was.

He said, "You should talk. You're still working."
It's true. She was wearing her garden gloves
and pants with muddy knees.

"Well, Eden's almost done for the season.
Bare ruined choirs in the arbor,
where late we walked."

"*Choirs*," he mused. "Is that a new word?"
She smiled. "How do you think
we should spell it?"

From a distance Earth was turning
into a masterpiece. God pondered a second
sun, so there'd never be a dark side.

"No," she reflected. "One noon is plenty,
and see how rich the blues are as light fades."
"Perhaps a moon then,

just a little one." And that
bit of tinkering was all they did
for the rest of the day.

Business

"I should have stepped in,"
God said, "when they began to barter
figs for sharpened stones."

"Don't blame yourself."
Mrs. God took the Lord's hand.
"People are still basically good."

They looked down
as a cluster of speculators
began to short the new armistice.

"You gave them manna.
That was brilliant." She remembered
the day people realized this heavenly bounty

could not be seized, hoarded,
and monetized. From a distance
she had watched the most ambitious

struggle beneath insane burdens,
only to find swarming maggots the next
morning, their inventory spoiled.

One by one they seemed to catch on.
But eventually the very same people
invented hedge funds.

"Maybe we can learn something
from them," Mrs. God suggested,
"and just stop caring."

First Love

After God created love he felt
himself swooning. "What is this?"
he cried out to Mrs. God.
"What have I done?
Is it a kind of music?"
"It bears a strong resemblance,"
she said softly, watching the warm sea
begin to rise and fall, as though
longing for the moon.
"Take slow, deep breaths," she advised,
"and it will pass."

But it didn't. All day God wandered
in Eden, on the verge of weeping.
The tree of the knowledge of good and evil
was in full bloom. He'd made it
self-pollinating, but now he changed
his mind and decided that to fruit,
a second tree must be planted nearby.
"Close, but not too close,"
Mrs. God, the horticulturalist, advised.
"The bees will find it."

Another evening, glorious among the clouds.
She was humming, mending something,
when God touched her shoulder.
"Yes," she said, smiling. "Yes,
it was a good day."

PART THREE

. . . in which we haggle
ourselves to sleep

Artificial Tears

Tears sometimes come in a bottle.
Twist it open and apply drops
several times daily
if you haven't enough of your own,
if you've begun to see light

where there is none,
on a humid night in the country,
black and brooding. Nothing.
And then a lightning strike.
But sometimes darkness

is the symptom: an ink spot, a stain,
a crow in the corn,
and a face you love stops smiling.
A temporary burning sensation
is normal. Perhaps

you'll see double, two worlds,
the woods twice as thick,
two hunter's moons,
one trailing the other. It may be
you're not blinking enough

or getting the sleep you need.
Bottled weeping: break the safety
seal, tip your head back, force
your eyes open, and let
the tears fall in.

I Heard You Come In

something like three
and I knew what it meant:
your vigil was over.
You'd stayed with your father day and night
in case he woke,
in case he came once more
to the surface, to the interface between worlds,
the hospital room with its enormous window;
came like a whale to break the glass sea
and take a deep breath,
and cast a living eye upon you
and roll, weedy and barnacled,
and go back down.
Thanks to morphine his face
betrayed nothing, not impatience, nor sorrow,
nor gratitude, nor fear, none of the passions
of a dying animal. His poor bony chest,
his nose and fingers half white, half blue,
his cheek stubble like a light frost—
we could stare all we wanted.
Thanks to morphine the door was easy
to open as we arrived and left.
It wasn't like someone being born,
the groaning, the leaky, bloody struggle
that ended with sad wails from the baby
and smiles elsewhere.
This was quiet, processional,
an orderly cell by cell evacuation
until the building stood empty
and the fire burned it down.

Pavement Ends

to my father on the anniversary of his death

At last the pavement ends.
Now if I lose your scent
I can follow your footprints.
You're still breathing in the fog,
your lungs ghostly and delicate
like white lilacs.

I don't care how many or what kind
have walked here, or run.
I only care about you,
your tracks fresh and firm,
as though you're nearly within reach.
Don't let me slow you down.
I will find you.

The Shoes of the Dead

Even here among the poor
the dead man's shoes found
no second master.
They strode no more together
into the sand, into the mountains.
They collected no more stones.
Their laces never tightened, their
tongues fell silent, their soles
were cool to the touch.
A left and a right, like gloves.
Human symmetries.
A first year and a last,
and neither required shoes.

A Last Time for Everything

Some marriages are rafts. I saw water between
The green logs. You could not have saved me.
—ROBERT BLY

Each time she peeled an orange
she thought of him,
dead almost six years now, settled law.
She described, pulling off the thick skin,
how she fed him, care-full,
as though this fruit were his first
solid food, how she removed
every bit of translucent membrane
from each crescent, leaving only
tiny tender vials of aromatic juice on his tray,
his last taste on earth.
Let it be sweet. Poor man.

When was the last time she set herself
against him? There were still times.
A skunk nest of old reasons, one needn't
get close to know where they are. Still
that final spring they talked,
tender days and nights, having shared
their only lives, having commingled
blood and money. When was the last time
he set himself against her?
Long before he was certain
he would never get out of bed again.

If it weren't for the kids.
Children were like the Hoover Dam,
strangling a river to create immense power
and a heavenly lake through which she
could look down to see
her old life, her maidenhood, that had drowned
as the water rose. Fathoms below
there remained a time and place
she couldn't forget, magnified by the waters.
She was still a girl down there, and free.
Then she met him,
and they were free together. Ah!

Luckily she loved work.
Sometimes if you work hard enough
you'll sleep. She was not, for example,
done planting trees. She found them
irresistible, the nursery a danger
like the animal shelter to someone
who loves saving lives
and work. Nothing was more stirring
than the green of new growth,
tender and trusting. She thought of him
every day, his green-gold eyes,
their old Bohemian mischief restored.
She could see his faults and his innocence
clearly in their children,
and their children.

Practice

Sometimes I practice being dead,
lying down alone, clearing out
all thoughts. I practice

being my father, whom I resemble,
closing my eyes and not breathing
until I can't help it.

I imitate the way he pretended
not to care. I stifle the same
panic until it drains

out of my fingertips, my tongue
too dry to moisten my lips.
Then I get up.

Phoebe

1.

Can't you hear that?
You tilted your head, hand cupped
around your ear, eyes closed.
At such times your face
never registers disappointment.
A phoebe cannot sing to you. Fact.
The little gray and black
flycatcher introduced itself
to the rest of the evening.

2.

I wonder if I'll ever love this house.
It isn't necessary that I do.
Someone used to. Someone
loved every brick. Our first summer here
we gave our daughter the best room.
I loved that summer;
the phoebe nested under the eaves
outside her window. We didn't paint
the west side till the young had fledged.
So many, and they all survived.

3.

What's beautiful?
One thing: the way a phoebe
hovers just above the grass:
Wings! The sun-glow through
spread feathers.
To care so little about gravity
that the Palisades, the vertical cliffs,
are "safe as houses."

4.

My father, when he was almost sixty,
began to plan his next life
which he filled with various jobs:
shrimp boat captain, staff writer
for the *Dick Van Dyke Show*,
hobo. In places like Chicago.
He'd never marry (no offense)
and he'd never join the army.
He'd never own a house.
Maybe just a mud and feather
nest somewhere for a summer,
then south in the fall.

5.

Certain sounds
are lost to you now, after years
near a hammer drill,
a Milwaukee Sawzall.
A phoebe calls: it's not necessary,
like supper and sleep.
It's a small tear in your shirt,
which you still wear.
It's not a whole life in two notes,
is it? It's not melodic.
It's information, a windblown claim,
a drop of rain that soon dries,
a gray stone giving its heat
to the evening.

They Live with Us

They live with us, the dead.
We take them places
as we used to take our children,
keeping them safe and fed.
Like children they sometimes wake us
with a touch on our shoulders
or just by standing next to the bed,
shivering, till we
wake up sweating in the dark.
There. We're conscious.
That's all they wanted.

Sometimes the dead just need to hear us
sigh for them, as a breeze
passes over moss. I never say no,
as I never could to the kids,
or speak the least ill of them.
Even now they are weighing
every word I write,
nodding, murmuring,
Of course, of course.

Recalled to Life

It was the age of wisdom, it was the age of foolishness.
—CHARLES DICKENS

They "courted" in their sixties, that's how formal it felt.
Dates: not the edible kind! Not unbearably sweet,
not at first. A paper calendar hung from a nail,
a ring around one day.
        When you draw a circle,
she said, you instinctively start at the top.
A careful decline, of course, then suddenly
you aren't just falling, you're going backwards.
At the bottom you force the ink on, because look,
the line is rising now, slightly atremble
so near the beginning.
        I haven't felt like this,
she said, since I was sixteen and had a terrible crush.
Up at the family cabin, she wandered,
staring at her cell phone for a signal, just one tower.
Her son will never understand, nor his daughter.
She tried the stony shore and waded into the lake,
waves to her thighs, phone tight to one ear,
finger in the other. A ring at last!
And there he was.

Walleye

Swift as a shadow, short as any dream;
Brief as the lightning in the collied night.
—*A MIDSUMMER NIGHT'S DREAM*

I forgot what we were fighting over,
but at last you gave up and drifted
into the green net.
Then the passion began anew
in the stern of the canoe,
your fins erect,
your gills gaping like saber cuts.
My husband shook his head no.
After all we'd been through
I couldn't keep you.
Men have always told me what to do.

I could hardly look at you,
tossing and turning.
How gold you were, how you shone,
as though you'd swallowed
rings and royal chains
and your entrails had forged them
into scales. You'd bent my rod tip
toward water, water, water . . .

You were both too big and too small:
in Minnesota, such are the limits,
such is the law, nuanced,
but structural, extending well below frost line
to rest upon the old black rock.
The law passes through us on its way
to the end of the universe.

We were paddling the Kawishiwi,
the *river of many beaver houses*,
those stick heaps gathered after
killing the little popple, accumulating
fresh white wooden femurs, beaver gnawed.
Underground a popple grove
is all the same tree, a nation of one,
a singular notion,
a discrete creation.
Popple is one idea in the world.
Another is the tooth of a beaver.

Another is my savageness.
Was it always there? Or is it just *you*?
We met and fell in love
over my lure, like Oberon and Titania.
You are the great king of the walleye
who could drink this river dry,
the potion of the Kawishiwi
that wakens our lust
for the next improbable creature we see.

You couldn't be measured.
No one could get a rope on you.
Between us there was no mercy —
I'd have killed you
but for the law. My husband
untangled you, not me.
He teased out my hook
like a referee. He gave you back
your Kawishiwi.

Wild Asters

for Laurie Hertzel

When the nights cool
then bloom the asters at the wild edge
of the graveyard.

More white than blue
this fall, half flower, half feather,
a study in modesty.

We haven't time for them,
not that they mind. We aren't the mower
nor the browsing deer.

They haven't time for us.
Quickly now, to seed before
the wind dies!

Brave Rabbits

for my nest mates

A hare stopped in the clover and swaying flower-bells, and
said a prayer to the rainbow, through the spider's web.
—ARTHUR RIMBAUD

We were convinced: either we would die
or we'd be fine. We'd beat this. All better,
a Band-Aid across the knee, dried tears.
And more life, running outside, letting
the screen door slap against the stop.

I wanted simply to hang up laundry
in the basement, to pin the children's socks
to the line. That would be Christmas,
to unwrap a thankless task
and finish with an empty basket.

Remember when your mother broke
her collarbone and wore a child's brace
(she had shrunk) and finally
the doctor said, "It will never heal.
She's too old." Yes, well.

We do have work: as cartographers
drafting maps of the wasteland
between health and death,
where days aren't made of hours
and socks have holes,

where brave rabbits freeze,
testing their composure
like suspects in a lineup,
appraised by hidden Beings
who are ravenous for any answer.

Brave Rabbits, a Second Look

People do get carried away.
Kindness is your genius.
Nothing else stops the roar.
Your insurance, will it pay?

(The only way to end war
is to require Allstate to cover
acts of it. But I digress—) My loves,
you made your peace,

waves at rest, stealing no thunder
from the sky, bringing in the wash,
the sea glass, in simple white,
smooth and common, to set among

the stones so that people like me
can pocket it and feel the world
isn't cheating. Oh, yes, our *diagnoses*,
our cargo. You make me strong. Enough.

A Marsh at Twilight

for Ann Jenkins

Last night's ice, the first this fall
melted by ten. It took till ten, but it happened.

If glass were really ice,
the windows would all be open again.

Remember when libraries had glass floors
and made us want to work there?

We'll be gone before the marsh is hard enough
to hold us up. But what if we stayed on?

Some days I can't bear to part
with one more thing: not the shoes

I used to run in, not the book I meant
to read (or write) nor the microwave onion

baker (forever unused) nor a pretty button
nor even the whine of June mosquitoes

at the edge of a blue marsh, drowning out the frogs.
Well, maybe that. What are the colors

of this moment? Is anything ever truly black
and nothing else?

The Second Half of the Night

Sometimes the second half of the night
begins just after lunch,
a stumble toward the sofa bathed
in sunlight.

The morning paper opens like a butterfly
to shade your eyes, and soon
all the stories written on its wings
seem old and fleeting.

Trouble is the Story of Man. The first
half of the night is your birthright.
The rest you must earn, a dollar an hour,
a modest living.

You'll never get rich this way, but you
would make a poor rich man.
Nor can you haggle yourself to sleep
as a miser can.

Sometimes those last hours are a solemn debt
you can't collect. Write them off,
one dream at a time, until
the morning light.

Cabbage Moth

I'm suddenly aware that the air
is crowded with small wings.
I have something to protect now:
the greens I tucked in,
telling them a story.

Once there was a garden where, to live,
nothing required the death of anything else,
where even the fragile were fearless.
We had just one infinite language
that sounded like Mozart
sung by a cabbage. To learn it
you only had to breathe.

How to master the wind
is every moth's spring obsession,
how to leave one's eggs
affixed to the perfect underleaf.
The dark spot on each white wing
is evidence of an entirely different life
that's over, that succeeded,
before this troubled one began.

Garden Gloves

By August we hardly know them.
Work made them ours alone.
Tugged on, often too late,
they tried to be braver than they felt.

But isn't that exactly
what we do for each other?
Let me hold your hands now.
Let the harm come to me.

Also by This Gardener

The yard and woods shared ferns,
but who owned the seven birches?
Deer that crossed the property line

became mine, before they strolled
up Harm's Way. The sun
tells when to plant and where

if you care about your yield,
and in which field will the spring
lambs learn their colors and become

numbers? Last season's mud
hardened on the shovel. I was raised
to hate that, to love order,

corn in mounds and mounds
in a row. I was taught to measure
the inches between fences.

But I learned to surrender.
Here are all my keys to the land:
this handful of seeds.

In the Ted Kooser
Contemporary Poetry series

Darkened Rooms of Summer:
New and Selected Poetry
Jared Carter

Rival Gardens: New and Selected Poetry
Connie Wanek

To order or obtain more information
on these or other University of Nebraska
Press titles, visit nebraskapress.unl.edu.

CPSIA information can be obtained
at www.ICGtesting.com
Printed in the USA
FFOW04n1758060316
22093FF